# Using Rubrics to Improve Student Writing

Grade 2

**REVISED EDITION**

Sally Hampton

Sandra Murphy

Margaret Lowry

The International Reading Association attempts, through its publications, to provide a forum for a wide spectrum of opinions on reading. This policy permits divergent viewpoints without implying the endorsement of the Association.

| | |
|---|---|
| *Executive Editor, Books* | Corinne M. Mooney |
| *Developmental Editor* | Charlene M. Nichols |
| *Developmental Editor* | Tori Mello Bachman |
| *Developmental Editor* | Stacey L. Reid |
| *Editorial Production Manager* | Shannon T. Fortner |
| *Design and Composition Manager* | Anette Schuetz |
| *Design and Production* | Progressive Information Technologies |

Cover photos: © 2008 Jupiterimages Corporation

The publisher would appreciate notification where errors occur so that they may be corrected in subsequent printings or editions.

**Library of Congress Cataloging-in-Publication Data**

Hampton, Sally.
    Using rubrics to improve student writing, grade 2 / Sally Hampton, Sandra Murphy, Margaret Lowry. — Rev. ed.
        p. cm.
    Includes bibliographical references.
    ISBN 978-0-87207-772-0
1. English language—Composition and exercises—Study and teaching (Elementary)—United States—Evaluation. 2. Second grade (Education)—United States—Evaluation. I. Murphy, Sandra. II. Lowry, Margaret. III. Title.
    LB1576.H233173 2009
    372.62'3044—dc22
                                                                2008030871

# About the Authors

**Sally Hampton** is a Senior Fellow for America's Choice, Inc. Previously she served as Senior Scholar at the Carnegie Foundation for the Advancement of Teaching and as the Director of English Language Arts and Deputy Director of Research and Development for New Standards. She has taught in both urban and rural classrooms and developed reading and writing programs. Most recently she worked with Lauren Resnick to produce *Reading and Writing With Understanding*, a volume that addresses comprehension and composing in grades 4 and 5.

**Sandra Murphy** is a Professor Emerita at the University of California, Davis. She is interested particularly in writing assessment and its impact on teachers and curriculum, reading comprehension, and critical perspectives on literacy.

**Margaret Lowry** is the Director of First-Year English at the University of Texas at Arlington. She teaches courses in writing and U.S. literature and participates in the training of graduate teaching assistants. Her research interests include composition pedagogies, teacher training, and women's autobiographical writings.

# About New Standards®

New Standards is a joint project of the Learning Research and Development Center at the University of Pittsburgh (Pennsylvania, USA) and The National Center on Education and the Economy (Washington, D.C., USA). From its beginning in 1991, New Standards was a leader in standards-based reform efforts. New Standards, heading a consortium of 26 U.S. states and 6 school districts, developed the New Standards® Performance Standards, a set of internationally competitive performance standards in English language arts, mathematics, science, and applied learning in grades 4, 8, and 10. New Standards also pioneered standards-based performance assessment, developing the New Standards® reference examinations and a portfolio assessment system to measure student achievement against the performance standards.

With support from the U.S. Department of Education, New Standards produced a collection of publications addressing literacy development, including the award-winning *Reading and Writing Grade by Grade*, as well as *Reading and Writing With Understanding*, *Speaking and Listening for Preschool Through Third Grade*, and a series on *Using Rubrics to Improve Student Writing* for kindergarten through fifth grade.

$\mathcal{W}$riting is hard work, and teaching children to write well is very hard work. Your commitment to this challenge is vital to the future success of all the students you teach, both while they are in school and later, when they become active members of their communities.

This book provides tools to help you teach writing. It contains information about written genres and specialized rubrics that emphasize writing strategies. It also includes a collection of student work with commentaries that explain the strengths and weaknesses of the examples.

Not all the student writing in this book is at standard. Instead, we have provided you with samples that are spread out along a continuum of performance, from work that is exceptional to work that falls considerably below what children at this grade level should be expected to produce. This continuum will allow you to identify similar performances from your students and let you see how far from—or close to—standard they are. The rubrics and commentaries have been designed to provide a formative assessment to help you plan instruction.

The students whose work is included here were fortunate to have been taught by dedicated professionals like you, teachers who helped them write with exuberance and purpose about what they knew, what they thought, and what they wondered. They are novice writers, to be sure, but their potential is obvious in their ability to employ writing strategies and techniques to communicate with their audience.

We can all be guided and inspired by the work that follows.

*Lauren B. Resnick*

Lauren B. Resnick
Codirector, New Standards
University of Pittsburgh

*Marc S. Tucker*

Marc S. Tucker
Codirector, New Standards
The National Center on Education and the Economy

# Acknowledgments

The rubrics, student writing, and commentaries contained in this document were all compiled during the 2001–2002 school year. They were the result of work done in kindergarten through fifth-grade classrooms that used the New Standards® performance standards, the New Standards® primary literacy standards, and America's Choice author and genre studies.

I would like to thank the many students, teachers, literacy coaches, and principals for their contribution to this document. The New Standards project acknowledges the work of the Noyce Foundation in the development of the rubrics.

*Sally Hampton*

Sally Hampton
Senior Fellow for Literacy
America's Choice, Inc.

# Introduction

## Formative Assessment in the Age of Accountability

In today's world, schools are being held accountable for student performance on state tests. Summative assessments of this kind provide useful information to the public and to policymakers. But the information they provide is of limited use to teachers, primarily because state assessment results arrive too late to effectively inform instruction. In this book we hope to help teachers develop an informed perspective about formative assessment and how that kind of assessment is an effective tool for instruction that fosters student learning.

There are clear differences between formative and summative assessments. Summative assessments sum up learning. They evaluate student performances in terms of where students are expected to be at the end of an instructional year or grading period.

Formative assessments, on the other hand, are intended to provide feedback and to guide instruction. Teachers who conduct formative assessments gather information about what their students know and are able to do at various points in time; using this information, they make decisions about what students need help with next. They also use this information to provide feedback to students. The best formative assessments, according to Paul Black and his colleagues, are those that provide effective feedback (see, for example, Black & Wiliam, 1998). Black describes the characteristics of such feedback as follows: First, effective feedback must be intelligible so that students can grasp its significance and use it both as a self-assessment tool and as a guide for improvement. Second, effective feedback must focus on particular qualities of the student's work. Third, effective feedback must provide advice about how to improve the work and set an achievable target. To these criteria we would add two caveats: First, effective feedback must evolve as students acquire new skills. Second, effective feedback about writing should not be generic; it should refer to particular genres and the elements and strategies associated with them.

## Learning About Genres

A genre is a rough template for accomplishing a particular purpose with language. It provides the writer and the reader with a common set of assumptions about what characterizes the text. So, for example, if the text is labeled a mystery story, there is an assumption that the story line will be built around some puzzle to be resolved or some crime to be solved. Likewise, when a piece starts off "Once upon a time…," there is an assumption that we will be reading or writing a fairy tale or a parody of a fairy tale. But if the first line of a text is "Whales are mammals," we expect a very different genre—a report of information instead of a story.

As Charles Cooper (1999) explains, writers shape texts to accomplish different purposes by using and adapting particular patterns of organization, by using particular techniques to develop the text, and by making particular language choices. Although there is a lot of variation from one text to another within the same genre, texts in a particular genre nevertheless follow a general pattern. As a result, readers develop expectations that enable them to anticipate where a text is going so they can make sense of it as they read. Writers know how to order and present thoughts in language patterns readers can recognize and follow.

Lack of genre knowledge will impair a student's academic success. The student who is required to produce a report but who does not know the expectations relative to report writing is immediately disadvantaged. That student must guess at how information might be ordered, what kind of stance/persona could be effective, how much information should be provided, and what level of specificity would be sufficient. By comparison, the student who is genre savvy and is aware of the various expectations attached to informational writing can choose which genre expectations to guide his or her writing, which to disregard, and if or where to vary the conventional pattern. This genre-savvy student enjoys a tremendous advantage over the first student.

Genre knowledge also supports reading comprehension. If children are familiar with the structure of a text, they can make predictions and understand the functions of text features such as dialogue, and so read more purposefully. Moreover, being familiar with the text structure also makes it easier for readers to internalize the information in a text. Students who understand the organizational pattern of a text can use this knowledge to locate key information, identify what is important and unimportant, synthesize information that appears in different locations within a text, and organize the information in memory. In general, making readers more aware of genre structure appears to improve comprehension, memory, and, thus, learning.

Several genres are fundamental to writing development in kindergarten through fifth grade. The four that are discussed in this book and the others in the grade-by-grade New Standards rubrics series are (1) narrative writing (sharing events, telling stories), (2) report of information (informing others), (3) instructions (instructing others about how to get things done), and (4) responding to literature. The characteristic features of each of these genres are presented in rubrics that describe different levels of performance.

In their current form, the rubrics in this book are not designed to be used with students. They are too complex, and their language is too abstract for children. However, the rubrics can easily serve as templates for guiding the development of grade-level-appropriate classroom rubrics that address elements and strategies. They are, in effect, end-of-the-year targets from which a teacher maps backward to plan instruction.

## What Makes a Rubric Good to Use With Students?

Rubrics can be developed and used in formative or summative ways. Typically, rubrics used in summative evaluation are short. They provide a minimum amount of detail so that scorers can quickly and efficiently assign a score to a piece of student writing. Rubrics used in summative assessment are also static, out of necessity. After all, only by using the same rubric can

you get comparative data in order to report trends over time. Further, they represent how students are expected to write at the end of a grading period. Summative rubrics don't provide information about the road along the way. Formative rubrics, on the other hand, trace patterns of development and focus on the particular.

### Focus on the Particular

The brevity required for efficient scoring and the static nature of summative rubrics fight against what teachers and students need to foster writing development. For example, it is not enough for a writer to be told that his or her writing is "well organized," a phrase commonly found on generic rubrics in state assessments. Such a global statement does not help the writer understand what it takes to make writing well organized. A more effective descriptor would be, "Clearly sequences events in the story and maintains control of point of view."

### Be Intelligible

Formative rubrics must also be meaningful to students. Ideally, they should grow out of the work of the classroom and represent a consensus about what constitutes good writing. They must be written in language that the students understand, language that is familiar. The goal is for students to be able to self-assess their writing in order to take on productive revisions and interact with peers in response groups or with the teacher in a conference. The language of the rubric should frame such interactions so that they are meaningful to everyone and grounded in the classroom culture.

### Set Targets and Offer Advice

Formative rubrics should set targets and offer advice. At each score level, a good rubric provides a list of criteria that defines performance at that level. Advancement to the next level (the target) comes about by refining the paper to match the criteria in the next score level. So, for example, if a student's paper is at score point 3 and that student wants a score point 4, the student must revise the paper to include all the elements for the higher score currently missing from the paper or must refine the way in which the elements and strategies in his or her paper are developed. Rubrics are not good tools for revision if the distinctions between score levels are set only by qualifiers such as "scant" detail, "some" detail, "adequate" detail, and "effective" detail. Better rubrics provide more definitive distinctions such as "no introduction," "an introduction that names the topic and provides at least minimal context," or "an introduction that names the topic, provides context, and generates reader interest." Better rubrics focus on the features and components of particular genres (for example, in narrative, character development, plot, dialogue, flashback). Such rubrics provide students and teachers with language to talk about the ways certain texts accomplish particular purposes. The rubrics presented in this book encompass both the genre elements and the strategies associated with each genre.

## Be Developed in a Classroom Setting

Students and teachers need formative rubrics that emerge from the teaching in a classroom and that specify work yet to be done. To learn about genres, students need to be engaged in active inquiry. Guided by their teachers, they can analyze texts of a published author, a peer, or their own work, and develop classroom rubrics as they examine the texts. The texts will serve as examples and inspiration. These classroom rubrics should be constructed as guidelines to improve student writing performance.

When rubrics are constructed as guidelines to improve performance, it is possible for a student, working alone or with a teacher, to use a rubric as a checklist—a rough approximation of what is in place and how well wrought these elements are. Once that is done, the student should be able to study the criteria at the next level to determine

### {Informational Writing} Non-fiction

| | 4 | 3 | 2 | 1 |
|---|---|---|---|---|
| Resources | Uses a variety of sources | Uses some sources | Uses a few sources | Uses only 1 source |
| Paraphrasing | Info is in your own words | Info is mostly in your own words | Some info in own words, some is copied | Plagiarizes info – does not use own words |
| Organization | Very clear beg., mid., and end. Has subtitles and paragraphs | Some clear beg., mid., and end. Some subtitles, some paragraphs | Very little org. of beg., mid., and end. Few subtitles, few paragraphs | No beg., mid., end. Out of order! No subtitles. One long paragraph |
| Graphics | Graphics on each page | Some graphics | Few graphics | No graphics or one graphic |
| Facts | Uses lots of facts to support big ideas | Has some facts organized into paragraphs | Has some facts but they are not organized logically | Usually only a list of facts |

*The above is an example of a classroom rubric, constructed jointly by a teacher and her students. This joint construction ensures a shared understanding about what constitutes good writing and about what "next steps" should guide instruction.*

what further work would need to be done for the writing to show significant improvement.

In some cases, such as when papers are almost at standard, a simple revision by the student is enough to sufficiently improve the quality of the work. The revision conference would have the teacher providing a reminder, such as, "Did you forget x?" or a suggestion, "Why not flesh out your central character's motivation a bit?" No instruction would be necessary; the writer would just need to be nudged a bit. But in other cases, to bring the paper "up to standard" would require significantly more than a nudge. Many papers signal a substantial need for instruction, time, and practice.

*Note: Implicit here are two assumptions. One, that it is the job of the teacher to enable the writer and not just "fix" the paper. And two, that learning to write takes time. In some cases, learning to use the elements that define the next higher score point might take up to a year!*

## Change With Instruction

Formative rubrics grow. Thoughtful teachers know that they have to move students from their initial performances in September to more refined performances at the end of the year. The instruction they provide will make this change possible. Consider the kindergarten students who begin school with no awareness of the conventions of print. When asked to write a story, they will likely draw a picture and perhaps include some random letters. After instruction, and with time, these students will begin to produce writing that moves from left to right, and top to bottom. They likely will copy words from word charts and play with phonetic spelling. Initial rubrics should celebrate this growth with criteria aimed at moving students forward one step at a time.

Older students, too, will improve with focused instruction and practice. Consider a beginning of the year third-grade classroom in which a teacher is doing a study on narration. The first rubric might have as few as three elements in order to represent what students initially know:

1. Has a beginning that interests the reader
2. Has a number of events that taken together tell a story
3. Has some sort of closure

The three-element rubric captures the essence of narrative and, hence, is complete. A more fully developed narrative rubric would also have some mention of transitions and probably some mention of detail. So, the rubric could easily grow from three to five descriptors, as the teacher provides the necessary instruction.

# Growing a Rubric

## Changing the Number of Levels

Just as the number of descriptors in a rubric may grow, so may the number of levels. Assume the teacher begins the year with a rubric that has three levels: meets the standard, "great writing"; approaches the standard, "O.K. writing"; and needs more work, "ready for revision." As fewer students produce work that falls below standard, the bottom distinctions can disappear (literally be removed/cut off/marked out). Then what was once work that "meets the standard" can become "approaching a higher standard." This can be determined by teacher and students collaboratively. Similarly, work that "met the standard" can now become "ready for revision." Growing a rubric like this—constantly reexamining how good work must be to earn the highest distinction—is a powerful way to highlight student *growth* in writing.

## Changing the Anchor Papers

In themselves, rubrics leave much room for ambiguity. They can be made more explicit by providing examples of what they describe. These examples are called *anchor* papers. When the words on the rubric remain unchanged, but the paper that illustrates the level of performance they describe changes, the rubric is said to be "recalibrated." An example will help here: Assume that the rubric simply states, "Has a beginning that engages the reader." The paper that initially illustrates that concept may have a simple opening sentence/ phrase ("Once upon a time there lived a king" or "On Saturday, I saw light"). If recalibrated, the anchor paper would provide a more complex beginning, for example: a paragraph or longer that sets a plot in motion, an example of dialogue that immediately creates reader interest, a description that is simply riveting (think of the beginning of *Maniac McGee*), or even the resolution of a story told as a flashback.

# Understanding These Rubrics

## Elements and Strategies

The rubrics in this book are divided into two parts. The first section delineates the elements that are fundamental to the genre, and the second section lays out the strategies writers frequently employ to enhance the genre.

This division of the rubric is intentional. The elements are of critical importance and are foundational to the genre. Until a writer can address the elements with some proficiency, an instructional focus on strategies is misguided. Yet, it is not unusual for instruction to skip from very basic work on introductions and conclusions to an emphasis on lifting the level of language in a piece, most often by inserting metaphors and similes. While figurative language can distinguish a good piece of writing, it cannot compensate for a fundamental lack of development. Think of the compulsories in an Olympic figure skating event. The skater must demonstrate proficiency performing the athletic stunts required by the judges before attempting the more creative dance moves that are also part of his or her repertoire. Genres, likewise, require the writer to address certain elements.

That is not to say that the strategies are unimportant. Frequently, they work with the elements to carry a reader through the text. Consider the work of dialogue in advancing the plot of a novel. The dialogue provides clues about who characters are and what motivates them. Dialogue also frequently helps a reader make transitions when there are scene changes or shifts in time. But a novel without a well-developed plot, well-developed characters, or some organizational frame will not be made whole simply with the inclusion of dialogue.

Too often, writing instruction in narrative focuses on leads and transitions to structure chronological ordering and on teaching strategies out of context (for instance, including dialogue for the sake of having dialogue, rather than as a strategy to develop character or advance the action). In many classrooms, not enough time is spent on the elements, the "compulsories" of genres. For this reason, the rubrics have been designed to emphasize both strategies and elements. When teachers use the rubrics to analyze students' strengths and weaknesses in order to plan instruction, they should first focus on the elements section. The strategies can be folded in instructionally as students begin to demonstrate awareness of the elements. In some cases, young writers will likely pick up strategies on their own through their reading and by appropriating text from favorite authors.

*Note: The lists of elements and strategies provided in these materials are foundational. They are not meant to be exhaustive or exclusive.*

Except at the kindergarten level, the scores for the New Standards rubrics are distributed across five levels:

- Score point 5: Work that exceeds the grade-level standard
- Score point 4: Work that meets the standard
- Score point 3: Work that needs only a conference
- Score point 2: Work that needs instruction
- Score point 1: Work that needs substantial support

## Score Point 5

Papers at this score point go well beyond grade-level expectations. What sets score point 5 papers apart is the level of sophistication brought to the text by the writer. Occasionally, this sophistication is reflected in the writer's syntax or vocabulary. Sometimes the sophistication is shown by a nuanced execution of writing strategies. Other times it may simply be the level of development that comes from the writer's deep understanding of the topic or the genre. In all cases, what distinguishes a score point 5 is writing development that goes beyond what the school curriculum has provided that writer. Performance at this level is exceptional, beyond what might be expected even after a year's program of effective instruction. This is not to say that students writing at score point 5 could not benefit from instruction. Even adult professional writers work to hone their craft. There are many strategies that a writer can learn and work to refine, and these should be the basis for the teacher's instructional plan for exceptional writers.

## Score Point 4

Papers at this score point illustrate a standards-setting performance. They are a full representation of the genre, though some features may be better executed than others.

Score point 4 papers grow out of good teaching, student effort, and quite likely a genre-specific curriculum. These papers "meet the standard" for what students should be able to accomplish if they receive effective instruction.

*Note: The criteria that define score points 5 and 4 are identical. This is intentional. What distinguishes a 5 from a 4 is not the presence or absence of a particular element or strategy. Rather, it is the overall quality of execution and the level of language the writer employs. The writers of score point 5 papers frequently also bring something to the text that may not be provided by instruction—a deep understanding or passion for the topic and the genre.*

## Score Point 3

Generally, the papers at score point 3 do not meet the standard for one of two reasons: (1) the writer did not include a necessary feature, such as a conclusion, or (2) the execution of a strategy was not well done. In either case, the writer of a paper at score point 3 is otherwise competent and needs only a conference to point out the paper's problem in order to revise it upward to a score point 4. The suggestions for improving the paper should come from the criteria at score point 4.

Score point 3 papers are not unusual with novice writers. Many young writers, for example, produce reports without an introduction because they assume that the title of their piece is sufficient to introduce the topic. Or they may not accommodate their readers by providing sufficient detail or a satisfactory ending. Such writers are completely capable of improving these inadequacies when they are pointed out in a teacher–student conference. It is these papers that represent score point 3. To achieve the target of score point 4, a teacher needs only to point out omissions from the criteria listed at score point 4 or the need for refinement in a revision.

## Score Point 2

The student writer of a score point 2 paper needs instruction in order to produce work that is up to standard. A quick read-through of the score point 2 paper makes obvious either that there are gaps in the writer's understanding of the genre features or that the writer simply has insufficient control over the strategy he or she is attempting. The instructional next steps are suggested by criteria at score point 4. However, it is almost certain that student work will pass through some of the inadequacies suggested by score point 3 before the writer can produce work that meets standard. The student producing writing at score point 2 needs instruction and practice with feedback. Deep understanding and resulting proficiency could take several months.

## Score Point 1

Papers that receive a score point 1 are representative of a writer who needs substantial support. The student writer at score point 1 may need extensive help

developing basic fluency and basic genre knowledge to move toward meeting the standard. The criteria at score point 4 outline a map for the student's development. To move from habitually producing work at a score point 1 to typically producing work at a score point 4 will require much support and time, perhaps as much as a year. Along with the classroom support from the teacher, students who write papers at score point 1 may require access to other kinds of safety nets, such as special programs, in order to make progress toward meeting the standard.

## How to Use These Rubrics

Research, as well as practical experience, demonstrate that within any single classroom the range of performance in writing and in children's knowledge of genres is wide. In any particular grade, some students' papers will look like the work of children in earlier grades, whereas the work of other students will appear more advanced. Even the work of a single child will show great variation from day to day because development does not progress smoothly forward in step-by-step increments. Moreover, skills that appear to be mastered are sometimes thrown into disarray as new skills are acquired.

We also know that students write some genres better than others. Research shows that young children typically have more experience with narrative genres than scientific or poetic genres. Research also shows that children are more successful handling the familiar structure of stories than the less familiar structure of arguments. One explanation for these differences may lie in the instruction about genres children receive, or do not receive, in school. Another explanation may be related to their experiences outside of school. If children have had infrequent exposure to particular genres, they will be less adept at writing and reading them than children who have had frequent exposure.

To use these rubrics, a teacher should first ask each student to produce a piece of writing specific to a particular genre. If the genre is narrative, the teacher might say, "I'd like you to write a story about…." If the genre is informational, the teacher might say, "I'd like you to write a report about…." If the genre is instructional writing, "I'd like you to write a paper explaining how to do something." Or if the genre is response to literature, "I'd like you to read this story/book/poem and then write a paper that explains what the author is saying." A response to literature by kindergarten students might be phrased as, "I'd like you to listen as I read and then write a response."

Once the student writing is in hand, the teacher should analyze individual performances with the appropriate genre rubric. This analysis will indicate what kinds of instruction are needed for students to gain the knowledge and skills required to produce work in that genre at score point 4 (meets the standard).

*Note: Making a judgment about proficiency on the basis of a single sample is always chancy. To have a better sense of a student's proficiency, it is always wise to look at several samples.*

It is almost certain that student work will not reflect the same level of proficiency for each element or strategy contained in the rubric. That is, a student writer may establish a strong orientation and context (score point 4), but develop character only weakly (score point 2). The student could make good use of dialogue (score point 4), but provide too few details (score point 2). In fact, most papers produced by novice writers are of this uneven quality.

The point of these rubrics is not to assign an overall score to student work, as one might do in a formal assessment, and certainly not to assign a grade. Rather, it is to highlight for teachers the characteristics of student work at different levels of performance so that appropriate instruction and feedback can be provided. Grading student writing is a necessity for teachers, and it is essential that the grades assigned reflect student performance relative to the genre elements and strategies. Grades can be derived from the classroom rubric. See the sample classroom rubric on page 3.

## How to Use the Papers and Commentary

Papers at each score point are representative of what work at that score level might look like. They are concrete examples of what the rubric describes. The commentaries describe the student writing in relation to the rubric. Teachers can use the papers and commentaries to calibrate the levels of performance of their own students. Comparing their students' work with the work in this book will highlight for teachers the various levels of proficiency among their students and facilitate instructional planning. Students in upper-elementary grades can study the papers as models of work that represent either a strong performance for a genre, or work that could be strengthened through revision. Teachers can use

the commentaries to scaffold discussion, and working together, teachers and students can construct classroom rubrics. A further use for the papers and commentaries is as the focus for teacher meetings where the goal is to establish a shared understanding of what good writing looks like.

In all cases, the commentaries have been written with the intention of honoring what is in place in the papers. Too often, student assessment focuses entirely on what is missing and what is poorly done. This genre-based approach to writing assumes that writing development is a layered process in which new learning builds over time upon what is already in place. The starting point is always first to identify the paper's strengths. In this manner, writing assessment is a positive, additive process, one that is also transparent and meaningful to students.

At the end of each of the commentaries for papers at score points 3, 2, and 1, there is a set of "next-step" suggestions. For score point 3 papers, the set is titled Possible Conference Topics; at score point 2, Next Steps in Instruction; and at score point 1, Roadmap for Development. These different titles are indicative of the kind and amount of support a student will need to produce work that meets the standard (for instance, a short conference at score point 3 versus extended instruction at score point 2). All of these next-step suggestions are simply that—suggestions. It may well be that other sets of suggestions could also work. However, the suggestions provided were drawn from an analysis of dozens of papers typical of that score point, as well as from an analysis of the particular paper described in the commentary. These suggestions were also derived from the rubric criteria at score point 4.

It should be emphasized that students at score point 2 and score point 1 will not move from these score levels without passing through the next higher score level(s). Writing proficiency takes time and practice. There will be some slow steps forward and some backsliding on the students' part. But these are novice writers, so patience, practice, and coaching should be part of any instructional plan.

This book has been designed with insight into the complexities of teaching writing. It includes student work as models and lists of rubric criteria as scales, two things that, according to George Hillocks (1984), research indicates will improve student writing if used appropriately. This book was drawn from the work of dedicated teachers and hard-working students. (To protect their privacy, names have been removed.) Admittedly, this is only one part of a comprehensive writing program, but it will serve well those teachers who use it to plan for student instruction.

The student papers in this book were chosen from more than 5,000 pieces written by students in many different elementary schools in several different school districts. The papers illustrate the range of abilities and performance of students at different grade levels from kindergarten through fifth grade, as well as ranges within grade levels. In the first year of the project, 3,586 students participated. Their teachers taught author and genre studies, and at the end of the year, the teachers collected portfolios of student writing. The examples in this book are drawn from these students' portfolios.

# Narrative

arrative is the genre most commonly associated with elementary schools. In fact, people assume that narrative, or more specifically, story, is the purview of our youngest students. To a large extent this assumption is logical. Elementary school is filled with story—picture books, show and tell, dramas, and basal readers. Children make sense of their lives and their worlds through story. Jerome Bruner (1985) tells us, "They [young children] are not able to…organize things in terms of cause and effect and relationships, so they turn things into stories, and when they try to make sense of their life they use the storied version of their experience as the basis for further reflection. If they don't catch something in a narrative structure, it doesn't get remembered very well, and it doesn't seem to be accessible for further kinds of mulling over."

Narratives have time as their deep structure. A narrative involves a series of events that can be plotted out on some sort of time line. The time span could be short, a few moments, or long, even across generations.

There are many kinds of narratives (frequently called subgenres): memoirs, biographies, accounts, anecdotes, folktales, recounts, mysteries, autobiographies, etc. Recount is a kind of narrative in which the teller simply retells events for the purpose of informing or entertaining. Anecdotes, on the other hand, generally include some kind of crisis that generates an emotional reaction—frustration, satisfaction, insecurity, etc. Stories, in contrast, exhibit a somewhat different pattern. A complication creates a problem, which then has to be overcome (the resolution). Stories are built of events that are causally linked (the events recounted share a cause–effect relationship). Think for a moment about stories. It is quite easy to say of them, "this happened because this happened, so this happened and that caused this to happen." Narrative accounts, by contrast, are comprised of a series of events that in total may or may not add up to anything significant other than the reader's sense of "this is how things went." It is a matter of "this happened and then this and then this and then this." Folktales take yet another form. Like other genres, different subgenres of narrative can serve different purposes, for example, to entertain or to make a point about what people should do, or about how the world should be.

The New Standards expectation for student writers around narrative requires that they be able to craft a narrative account, either fiction or nonfiction, that does the following: establishes a context; creates a point of view; establishes a situation or plot; creates an organizing structure; provides detail to develop the event sequence and characters; uses a range of appropriate strategies, such as dialogue; and provides closure.

## Orientation and Context

As it relates to narrative, orienting the reader and providing context usually involves bringing readers into the narrative (situating them somehow in the story line) and engaging them.

There are many ways to do this, of course, but among the most common strategies are

- Introducing a character who is somehow interesting
- Establishing a situation that intrigues or startles a reader
- Situating a reader in a time or place
- Having a narrator speak directly to the reader in order to create empathy or interest

From this initial grounding, writers can begin to develop the event sequence of their narratives.

## Plot Development and Organization

The organization of narrative is not necessarily a straightforward chronological ordering of events. Consider just a few variations. Narratives frequently are organized as the simultaneously ongoing, unfolding of events in the lives of multiple persons or fictional characters. The end of such a narrative requires that several or all of these persons' or characters' lives come together. In some narratives, the sequence of events may be altered to create interest, so the writer may use flashbacks and flash-forwards to move the characters around in time or to create a "backstory" of the events leading up to the story. Stories within a story are another commonly used device. Mystery stories often are organized by laying out an initiating event (crime), and then providing a series of clues and several false resolutions before the truth is finally revealed. Newspaper stories traditionally flow from the standard "who, what, where, when, why, how?" of an introductory paragraph. Memoir is organized around a single event or series of events that sum up the essence of who someone is, or was, and what values and heritage shaped that person. Biography and autobiography usually begin with birth and move through early years, adolescent years, and late years of someone's life. The diversity of narrative genres, as well as the myriad ways in which they can be developed, serve to remind us of the various options writers have for communicating with readers.

In general, however, narratives are often organized in such a way that some event precipitates a causally linked series of further events, which in some way is ultimately resolved. Episodes share a relationship to each other and usually are built around a problem and emotional response, an action, and an outcome. Nuanced plotting frequently involves subplots, built through episodes, and shifts in time. The classic plot structures for conflict are man vs. man, man vs. society, man vs. nature, and man vs. self.

Although children and adults may tell complicated narratives, it is important to remember that they also tell simple recounts. Recounts tell what happened, and organization is based on a series of events that all relate to a particular occasion. Children often recount personal narratives about school excursions or particularly memorable events in their lives—their immigration to America, the death of a cherished pet, the birth of a sister, and so on. In recounts, sometimes there is not an initiating event; rather, writers present a bed-to-bed story that retells the mundane events of the day.

Adult writers use a variety of methods to develop event sequences and their settings. They typically develop settings by providing details about place, colors, structures, landscape, and so on. They use several techniques to manage event sequences and time, including flashbacks and flash-forwards, forecasting, and back stories. They sometimes manipulate time by compressing or expanding it, that is, by providing pacing. They use dialogue and interior monologue purposefully to advance the action. During the elementary school years, children are just beginning to master these techniques.

Because narratives are based on events in time, writers also often use linking words that deal with time and the organization of events (then, before, after, when, while). When people recount events, they often refer to the specific times when events happened (yesterday, last summer). As children mature, their repertoire of temporal signals develops, from simple transition words (then, after, before) to more complex phrases ("At the time...") and clauses ("Before he went in the house...").

## Character/Narrator Development

Adult writers use a variety of techniques to develop characters, and in some cases, the persona of the narrator. They describe their physical characteristics, their personalities, their actions and gestures, their emotional reactions to events, and through dialogue and internal monologue, their internal motivations and goals. Whether narratives include real people or fictional characters, the personalities, motivations, and reactions of the narrator and the characters are often central to the development of the narrative. When children develop characters, some are "stock characters" that regularly inhabit children's stories, such as the mean teacher, the school bully, and the wicked witch. Other characters are more fully and uniquely developed through description, dialogue, and other narrative techniques.

Although children may produce narratives in which fictional characters are fairly well developed, they are less likely to develop the persona of the narrator. And, when they are producing simple recounts of events in their lives, neither the people in their narrative nor the persona of the narrator may be particularly well developed. In simple recounts, the focus is more likely to be on what people did than on their motives or reactions.

## Closure

Writers bring closure to narratives in a variety of ways. Structurally, they achieve closure by providing a resolution to a problem (or a failed resolution). But they also provide closure with a variety of overt signals—with evaluations that inform the reader what the narrator thought about the events, with comments that serve to tie up loose ends in the narrative or bridge the gap between the narrative and the present, and with typical ending markers such as "the end" and "they all lived happily ever after." As children mature, their strategies for providing closure become more sophisticated and their repertoire of strategies more broad.

## Narrative in Second Grade

By second grade, students typically relate several incidents and events in their narratives. Some students, however, may just mention events but not develop them ("Todad, our class went to the Muzzi's Farm and corn Maze. It wus fun. We first, got a pumpkin. Afterward, we went in the maze."). They may produce writing that is simply framed by initiating and closing incidents, and the sequence may not always be clear.

They may also omit conclusions, simply stopping or ending with a simple evaluative statement ("Me and my dad made a tank it is yellow and black we worked on it for 2 days it was fun making a tank.").

Students who meet the standard in second grade develop incidents and events with description and dialogue ("I got to go on the space mountain ride. My friends asked me if I wanted to go on it, but I said "no," because I thought it was a scary ride. But, when they asked me a second time, this time I said "Yes!" When I got in the seat, there was room for only one passenger.... The ride started.... In the middle of the ride I felt happy...."). They also show a growing ability to manage and signal chronological sequence with temporal words, phrases and clauses ("when"; "then"; "now"; "At the end..."; "When I was there..."), and react to events, telling not only what happened, but what the character or person thought or felt about it ("That scared me a little bit, because usally I sit with my mom or dad..."; "They were surprised...").

Writers who meet the standard also provide conclusions, sometimes with simple concluding statements ("At the end, my mom and my friends sang 'Happy Birthday To You' to me. Then you know what's next. Cake and presents!"), and sometimes with formal markers, or both ("Then the parents said it was time to go. The End.").

# Narrative Rubrics Elements

| | 5<br>Exceeds Standard* | 4<br>Meets Standard |
|---|---|---|
| **Orientation and Context** | • Establishes a context (e.g., time, place, or occasion). | • Establishes a context (e.g., time, place, or occasion). |
| **Plot Development and Organization** | • Produces writing that reflects a plan about where in a series of incidents or events the story should start and stop.<br>• Develops a series of incidents or events. | • Produces writing that reflects a plan about where in a series of incidents or events the story should start and stop.<br>• Develops a series of incidents or events. |
| **Character/ Narrator Development** | • Uses specific details about characters.<br>• Develops character internally as well as externally (e.g., the writer tells not only what happened to a character, but what the character wondered, remembered, hoped). | • Uses specific details about characters.<br>• Develops characters internally as well as externally (e.g., the writer tells not only what happened to a character, but what the character wondered, remembered, hoped). |
| **Closure** | • Provides a conclusion.<br>• May react to, comment on, evaluate, sum up, or tie incidents together (e.g., "I wondered…"; "I thought…"; "it was great"; "It was the best birthday ever."). | • Provides a conclusion.<br>• May react to, comment on, evaluate, sum up, or tie incidents together (e.g., "I wondered…"; "I thought…"; "it was great"; "It was the best birthday ever."). |

| | 3<br>Needs Revision | 2<br>Needs Instruction | 1<br>Needs Substantial Support |
|---|---|---|---|
| **Orientation and Context** | • Establishes a simple context (e.g., time, place, or occasion). | • Establishes a simple context (e.g., time, place, or occasion). | • Establishes a simple context (e.g., time, place, or occasion). |
| **Plot Development and Organization** | • Produces writing that reflects a plan about where in a series of incidents or events the story should start and stop.<br>• Recounts a simple chronology of incidents or events. | • Produces writing that is typically framed by initiating and closing incidents, though the sequence may not be clear. | • Produces writing that is typically framed by initiating and closing incidents though the sequence may not be clear.<br>• Typically lists, but does not develop, incidents or events. |
| **Character/ Narrator Development** | • May provide little, if any, character development. | • Typically provides little, if any, character development. | • Typically provides little, if any, character development. |
| **Closure** | • May simply stop.<br>• May provide a simple evaluative comment (e.g., "It was fun."). | • May simply stop.<br>• May provide a simple evaluative comment (e.g., "It was fun."). | • May simply stop.<br>• May provide a simple evaluative comment (e.g., "It was fun."). |

*The criteria that define score points 5 and 4 are identical. This is intentional. What distinguishes a 5 from a 4 is not the presence or absence of a particular element or strategy. Rather, it is the overall quality of execution and the level of language the writer employs. Writers of score point 5 papers bring something to the text that may not be provided by instruction—a deep understanding or passion for the topic and the genre.

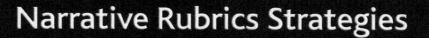

# Narrative Rubrics Strategies

| | 5<br>Exceeds Standard* | 4<br>Meets Standard |
|---|---|---|
| Detail | • Uses details to describe incidents and people. | • Uses details to describe incidents and people. |
| Dialogue | • Dialogue, if present, advances the action or develops character. | • Dialogue, if present, advances the action or develops character. |
| Other | • Uses some simple form of literary language (e.g., "Ding Dong! The doorbell rang."). <br>• Uses transition words, phrases, and clauses (e.g., "When they took my tonsils out…"). <br>• Frequently incorporates drawings. | • Uses some simple form of literary language (e.g., "Ding Dong! The doorbell rang."). <br>• Uses transition words, phrases, and clauses (e.g., "When they took my tonsils out…"). <br>• Frequently incorporates drawings. |

| | 3<br>Needs Revision | 2<br>Needs Instruction | 1<br>Needs Substantial Support |
|---|---|---|---|
| Detail | • Uses details to describe incidents and people. | • Produces writing that contains few details. | • Produces writing that contains little or no detail. |
| Dialogue | • May attempt the use of dialogue. | • May attempt the use of dialogue. | • Typically does not attempt the use of dialogue. |
| Other | • May use some simple form of literary language. <br>• Uses transition words, phrases, and clauses. <br>• Frequently incorporates drawings. | • May use some simple form of literary language. <br>• Uses simple transition words and phrases. <br>• Frequently incorporates drawings. | • May use some simple form of literary language. <br>• Uses simple transition words and phrases. <br>• Frequently incorporates drawings. |

*The criteria that define score points 5 and 4 are identical. This is intentional. What distinguishes a 5 from a 4 is not the presence or absence of a particular element or strategy. Rather, it is the overall quality of execution and the level of language the writer employs. Writers of score point 5 papers bring something to the text that may not be provided by instruction—a deep understanding and/or passion for the topic and the genre.

# Score Point 5

## Narrative Student Work and Commentary: "The Football Piñata"

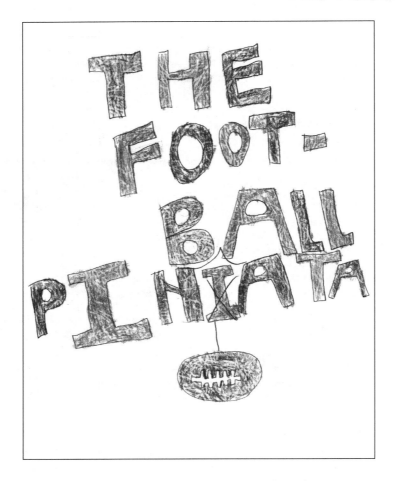

This lively piece describes the narrator's birthday party and focuses on the big event of the party: the football piñata. The piece includes an appropriate series of events and elaborates on important moments during the day. "The Football Piñata" exceeds the standard for narrative writing at second grade.

The writer establishes a context for the piece in the opening pages by describing his surprise when he opens the door and people are there for his party ("Ding Dong! The doorbell rang. I ran quickly to the door to see who it was, I opened it and—SURPRISE!!!").

The piece follows a series of events that reflect a plan about where the story should stop and start and what events to include. The writer begins the story by describing his surprise, and continues by describing the setting (his dirty shirt and the stinky garage) and the most important events at the party (the piñata and the kids' excitement over cake and presents). The writer paces the narrative effectively, creating suspense about when the piñata will break.

The piece includes specific details that reveal the characters' motives and describe the scene for readers. For instance, the writer describes how he felt during the party ("I can't believe my mom let me dress like that!"), and he gives details about important moments ("Candy, tons of candy, (and little toys), exploded out of the piñata and fell to the floor.").

The piece concludes by asking readers to guess what happened next in the party: "Then you know what's next. Cake and presents!"

# Score Point 5 *continued*

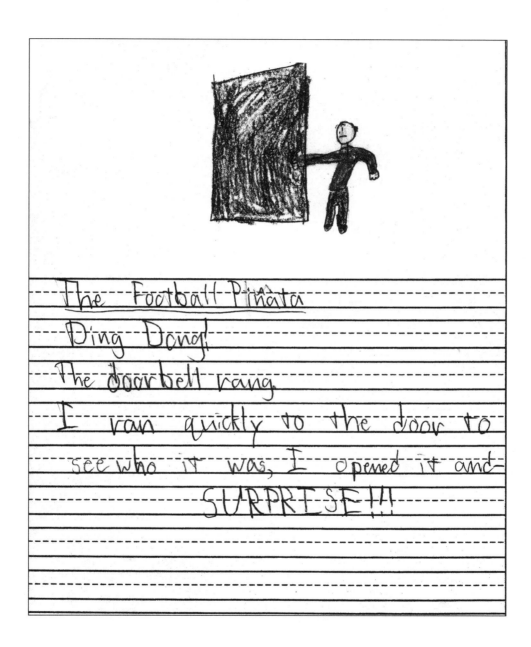

The Football Piñata

Ding Dong!
The doorbell rang.
I ran quickly to the door to
see who it was, I opened it and
SURPRISE!!!

This writer uses dialogue effectively to advance the action and reveal the characters' motivations. For instance, the kids interrupt the mom with a cheer even before she completes her sentence about cake, and their interruption reflects their excitement.

The piece includes literary language ("With one mighty strike she split the piñata in two.") and uses transition words to guide the reader ("Now it was my turn.").

# Score Point 5 continued

It was all my friends!
Here for my birthday party!
"Come in!" I excitedly shouted.
"Come in and have some fun!"
Right now I had messy hair
and a dirty shirt. I can't
believe my mom let me dress
like that!

After a while I thought
the time was coming. And it
was.
The piñata. The football piñata.
"I think it's time for the
piñata guys," I said in a
wonderingly way. "Lets go into
the garage." Once we got into
the garage, everyone slowly said
"pe-ew!"

# Score Point 5 continued

Like all garages, they're stinky.
But ours is really stinky! I think
it's because there's cat food all
over the floor, or because my
dad left open a can of stinky
paint. At that moment something caught our eyes. It was
hanging from the ceiling. We
looked up and saw a piñata

the shape and colors of a football.
"We are going in order from youngest
to oldest for who goes first on
hitting the piñata," my mom
explained. "Now everybody get in line!"
We all got in line from youngest
to oldest. After that, mom shouted
"Go!" My brother struck the
piñata hard three times. Now there
was a tiny hole in the piñata.
Now it was my turn.

# Score Point 5 *continued*

I struck the tiny hole on the piñata so hard that a jolly rancher fell out. I droped the candy into my bag. I'm the first one to get candy! I hit the piñata again. This time I think I hit the weak spot. I hit the piñata on the same spot. Now there was a gigantic hole in

the piñata. We all hit the piñata three times each until it was my sisters turn. With one mighty strike she split the piñata in two. Candy, tons of candy (and little toys), exploded out of the piñata and fell to the floor. We all picked up the goodies and draped them into our bags. "That's a very good hit, Jenny!" my mom exclaimed. "Now lets go have some cake

# Score Point 5 *continued*

and open some-." All of a sudden there was a big "YEAH!" That was the sound of us rushing to the dining room. "But I didn't finish my sentence!" my mom called. "Oh well." It was a really great day. At the end, my mom and my friends sang "Happy Birthday To You" to me. Then you know what's next.

Cake and presents!

# Score Point 5 *continued*

## Assessment Summary: "The Football Piñata"

| ELEMENTS | | |
|---|---|---|
| | **Exceeds Standard** | **Commentary** |
| **Orientation and Context** | • Establishes a context (e.g., time, place, or occasion). | The writer establishes a context for the piece in the opening pages by describing his surprise when he opens the door and people are there for his party ("Ding Dong! The doorbell rang. I ran quickly to the door to see who it was, I opened it and—SURPRISE!!!"). |
| **Plot Development and Organization** | • Produces writing that reflects a plan about where in a series of incidents or events the story should start and stop.<br>• Develops a series of incidents or events. | The piece follows a series of events that reflect a plan about where the story should stop and start and what events to include. The writer begins the story by describing his surprise, and continues by describing the setting (his dirty shirt and the stinky garage) and the most important events at the party (the piñata and the kids' excitement over cake and presents). The writer paces the narrative effectively, creating suspense about when the piñata will break. |
| **Character/ Narrator Development** | • Uses specific details about characters.<br>• Develops character internally as well as externally (e.g., the writer tells not only what happened to a character, but what the character wondered, remembered, hoped). | The piece includes specific details that reveal the characters' motives and describe the scene for readers. For instance, the writer describes how he felt during the party ("I can't believe my mom let me dress like that!"), and he gives details about important moments ("Candy, tons of candy, (and little toys), exploded out of the piñata and fell to the floor."). |
| **Closure** | • Provides a conclusion.<br>• May react to, comment on, evaluate, sum up, or tie incidents together (e.g., "I wondered…"; "I thought…"; "it was great"; "It was the best birthday ever."). | The piece concludes by asking readers to guess what happened next in the party: "Then you know what's next. Cake and presents!" |
| STRATEGIES | | |
| | **Exceeds Standard** | **Commentary** |
| **Detail** | • Uses details to describe incidents and people. | See previous commentary. |
| **Dialogue** | • Dialogue, if present, advances the action or develops character. | This writer uses dialogue effectively to advance the action and reveal the characters' motivations. For instance, the kids interrupt the mom with a cheer even before she completes her sentence about cake, and their interruption reflects their excitement. |
| **Other** | • Uses some simple form of literary language (e.g., "Ding Dong! The doorbell rang.").<br>• Uses transition words, phrases, and clauses (e.g., "When they took my tonsils out…").<br>• Frequently incorporates drawings. | The piece includes literary language ("With one mighty strike she split the piñata in two.").<br>The writer uses transition words to guide the reader ("Now it was my turn."). |
| *Note: The commentary highlights the elements and strategies in the student paper, focusing on how well the paper addresses the totality of the elements and strategies rather than on whether each is included.* | | |

# Score Point 4

## Narrative Student Work and Commentary: "My Ride on Space Mountain"

In "My Ride on Space Mountain," the writer describes his hesitation to ride on Space Mountain and the experience of the ride; the piece is a good example of narrative. The writer recounts a chronology of events, describes the main character's feelings and motives, and uses transition phrases to guide the reader through the story. This piece meets the standard for narrative writing at second grade.

The writer establishes a context with the piece's opening sentences ("A long time ago I went on an awesome trip to Florida. when I was there I went to Dinsey world.").

The writer produces writing that reflects a plan: After he sets the scene, he describes his hesitation to ride on Space Mountain and then tells about what happened on the ride.

The writer develops the main character by describing his feelings, such as his fear about not being able to sit next to his parents on the ride ("That scared me a little bit, because usally I sit with my mom or Dad."). His description of his hesitation to get on the ride also helps readers understand his motivations and fears.

The writer provides a sense of closure by describing a conversation he had after the ride and with the sentence, "Then the parents said it was time to go."

The piece includes details about the setting ("I turned around to see my Dad and I saw part of his shirt glowing.").

# Score Point 4 *continued*

A long time ago I went on an awesome trip to Florida. when I was there I went to Dinsey world.

The writer uses dialogue to describe the situation ("My Dad said how are you doing I said 'It's a little bumpy.'").

The piece includes literary language ("A long time ago") and transition phrases ("When I got in the seat…" and "In the middle of the ride…"). The phrases help pace the narrative by guiding the reader from one scene to the next.

# Score Point 4 *continued*

Me

I got to go on the space mountain
ride. My friends asked me if I
wanted to go on it, but I said
"No" because I thought it was
a scary ride. But, when they asked
me a second time, this time I
said "yes!"

raster

when I got in the seat
there was room for only one
passenger. That scared me
a little bit, because usally I
sit with my mom or Dad.
my Dad sat behind me.

# Score Point 4 *continued*

The ride started and I felt happy. The seats were comfortable and we were moving slowly. It started to speed up and then I got a little scared. It was dark and I kept thinking that we were going down.

In the middle of the ride I felt happy. I turned around to see my Dad and I saw part of his shirt glowing. My Dad said how are you doing I said It's a little bumpy.

# Score Point 4 *continued*

when we got off the
ride we saw the others
I said "Hi." they said
"we were on a different
ride." Then the parents
said it was time to go.

the end

# Score Point 4 *continued*

## Assessment Summary: "My Ride on Space Mountain"

| ELEMENTS | | |
|---|---|---|
| | **Meets Standard** | **Commentary** |
| **Orientation and Context** | • Establishes a context (e.g., time, place, or occasion). | The writer establishes a context with the piece's opening sentences ("A long time ago I went on an awesome trip to Florida. when I was there I went to Dinsey world."). |
| **Plot Development and Organization** | • Produces writing that reflects a plan about where in a series of incidents or events the story should start and stop.<br>• Develops a series of incidents or events. | The writer produces writing that reflects a plan: After he sets the scene, he describes his hesitation to ride on Space Mountain and then tells about what happened on the ride. |
| **Character/ Narrator Development** | • Uses specific details about characters.<br>• Develops characters internally as well as externally (e.g., the writer tells not only what happened to a character, but what the character wondered, remembered, hoped). | The writer develops the main character by describing his feelings, such as his fear about not being able to sit next to his parents on the ride ("That scared me a little bit, because usally I sit with my mom or Dad."). His description of his hesitation to get on the ride also helps readers understand his motivations and fears. |
| **Closure** | • Provides a conclusion.<br>• May react to, comment on, evaluate, sum up, or tie incidents together (e.g., "I wondered…"; "I thought…"; "it was great"; "It was the best birthday ever."). | The writer provides a sense of closure by describing a conversation he had after the ride and with the sentence, "Then the parents said it was time to go." |

| STRATEGIES | | |
|---|---|---|
| | **Meets Standard** | **Commentary** |
| **Detail** | • Uses details to describe incidents and people. | The piece includes details about the setting ("I turned around to see my Dad and I saw part of his shirt glowing."). |
| **Dialogue** | • Dialogue, if present, advances the action or develops character. | The writer uses dialogue to describe the situation ("My Dad said how are you doing I said 'It's a little bumpy.'"). |
| **Other** | • Uses some simple form of literary language (e.g., "Ding Dong! The doorbell rang.").<br>• Uses transition words, phrases, and clauses (e.g., "When they took my tonsils out…").<br>• Frequently incorporates drawings. | The piece includes literary language ("A long time ago").<br>The piece includes transition phrases ("When I got in the seat…" and "In the middle of the ride…") that help pace the narrative by guiding the reader from one scene to the next. |
| *Note: The commentary highlights the elements and strategies in the student paper, focusing on how well the paper addresses the totality of the elements and strategies rather than on whether each is included.* | | |

# Score Point 3

## Narrative Student Work and Commentary: "My Tonsils"

In "My Tonsils," the writer tells the story of having his tonsils removed. This lengthy piece includes a chronological list of the events surrounding his operation, and it is, in essence, a "bed-to-bed" account of his operation. This piece approaches, but does not meet, the standard for narrative at second grade.

The writer begins with his entry into the hospital at 5:00 a.m., describes what happened in the hospital, and ends with his return home and his inability to eat solid foods. The piece ends abruptly with the narrator asking for something to eat.

The piece is made up of a chronology of events marked by transition words ("Frist I went to a room where there were kids playing…" and "Then the doctor came…"). The events are all given equal weight (for instance, eating a popsicle after the surgery is described in the same way as being wheeled into surgery), and the writer does not develop the character by describing his internal thoughts, feelings, or motivations.

The piece includes dialogue between the boy and his parents. The piece ends with dialogue ("'here you can have some jello!' said my dad."), but the dialogue does not provide closure to the piece. The final page is a drawing of Stanford Hospital.

The writer includes specific information about the hospital setting ("There was a blood pressure mashine and fore chairs…"), but those details do not help develop character or plot.

# Score Point 3 *continued*

When they took my tonsils out
I went to the hospital at
5 in the mornig. Frist I went
to a room where there were
kids playing and lots of toys.
Then the doctor came ①

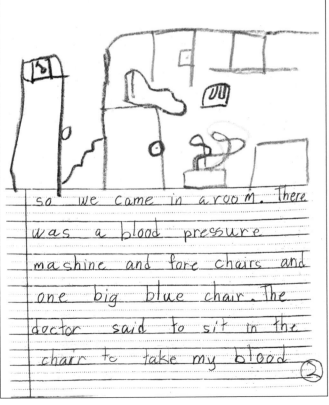

so we came in a room. There
was a blood pressure
mashine and fore chairs and
one big blue chair. The
doctor said to sit in the
chair to take my blood ②

# Score Point 3 *continued*

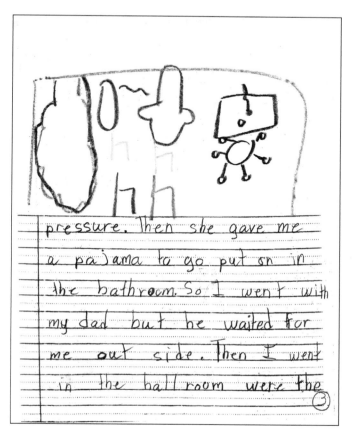

pressure. Then she gave me a pajama to go put on in the bathroom. So I went with my dad but he waited for me out side. Then I went in the ball room were the ③

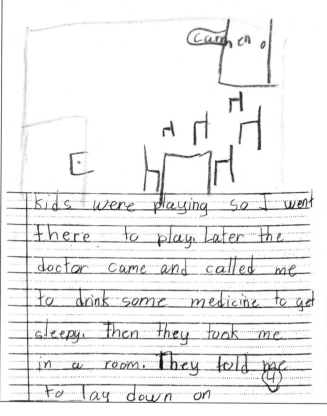

kids were playing so I went there to play. Later the doctor came and called me to drink some medicine to get sleepy. Then they took me in a room. They told me to lay down on ④

# Score Point 3 *continued*

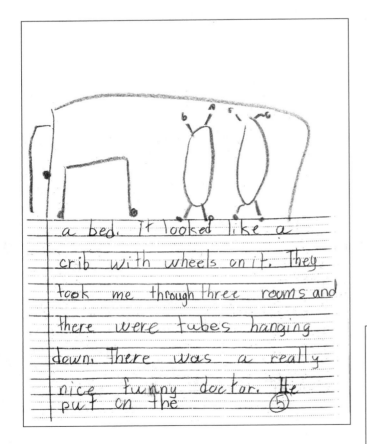

a bed. It looked like a crib with wheels on it. They took me through three rooms and there were tubes hanging down. There was a really nice funny doctor. He put on the ⑤

anestheia so I can fall asleep. When I woke up my dad was there. then he took a picher of me. Then he went some where. Later a doctor came with my ⑥

# *Score Point* **3** *continued*

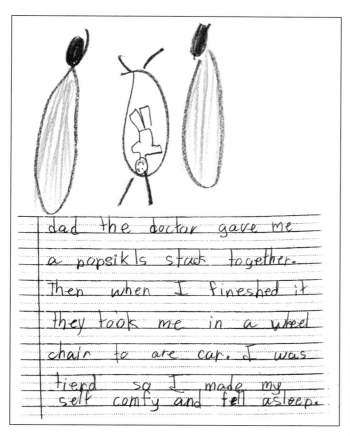

dad the doctor gave me
a popsikls stack together.
Then when I fineshed it
they took me in a wheel
chair to are car. I was
tierd so I made my
self comfy and fell asleep.

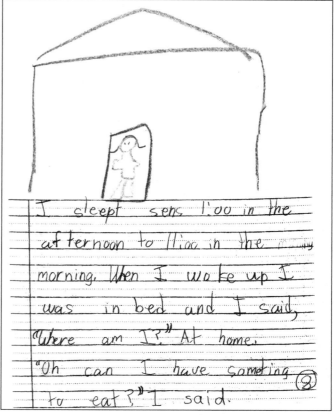

I sleept sens 1:00 in the
afternoon to 11:00 in the
morning. When I woke up I
was in bed and I said,
"Where am I?" At home.
"Oh can I have someting
to eat?" I said.

# Score Point 3 *continued*

"Yes but you can't have spice or hard or not too hot... oh here you can have some jello!" said my dad.

Score Point **3** *continued*

## Assessment Summary: "My Tonsils"

| ELEMENTS | | |
|---|---|---|
| | **Needs Revision** | **Commentary** |
| **Orientation and Context** | • Establishes a simple context (e.g., time, place, or occasion). | The writer begins with his entry into the hospital at 5:00 a.m. |
| **Plot Development and Organization** | • Produces writing that reflects a plan about where in a series of incidents or events the story should start and stop.<br>• Recounts a simple chronology of incidents or events. | The writer describes what happened in the hospital and ends with his return home and his inability to eat solid foods. The piece is made up of a chronology of events marked by transition words ("Frist I went to a room where there were kids playing..." and "Then the doctor came..."). The events are all given equal weight (for instance, eating a popsicle after the surgery is described in the same way as being wheeled into surgery). |
| **Character/ Narrator Development** | • May provide little, if any, character development. | |
| **Closure** | • May simply stop.<br>• May provide a simple evaluative comment (e.g., "It was fun."). | The piece ends abruptly with the narrator asking for something to eat. |
| STRATEGIES | | |
| | **Needs Revision** | **Commentary** |
| **Detail** | • Uses details to describe incidents and people. | The writer includes specific information about the hospital setting ("There was a blood pressure mashine and fore chairs."), but those details do not help develop character or plot. |
| **Dialogue** | • May attempt the use of dialogue. | The piece includes dialogue between the boy and his parents. The piece ends with dialogue ("'here you can have some jello!' said my dad."), but the dialogue does not provide closure to the piece. |
| **Other** | • May use some simple form of literary language.<br>• Uses transition words, phrases, and clauses.<br>• Frequently incorporates drawings. | The final page is a drawing of Stanford Hospital. |
| *Note: The commentary highlights the elements and strategies in the student paper, focusing on how well the paper addresses the totality of the elements and strategies rather than on whether each is included.* | | |

## Possible Conference Topics

The writer will benefit from a conference to discuss developing characters by describing their thoughts, feelings, and motivations, and providing a conclusion at the end of the story.

# Score Point 2

## Narrative Student Work and Commentary: "The cone mazze"

The cone mazze

"The cone mazze" tells the story of the writer's field trip with his class. The piece describes an assortment of activities that took place during the field trip, but the events are not arranged in a particular order. The writer of this piece needs instruction in order to meet the second-grade standard for narrative.

The writer creates a context by beginning with the sentence, "Todad, our class went to the Muzzi's Farm and corn Maze."

The piece describes many of the events of the field trip (such as getting pumpkins, entering the maze, and playing in a haystack), but the sequence of events is not clear. For instance, the reader moves from discussing the maze to the carpool, but the shift in topic is hard to follow, and the connection between the two events is not clear.

The piece does not include a closing statement; it simply stops.

The writer uses transition words such as "First" and "Afterward" to help create coherence.

# Score Point 2 *continued*

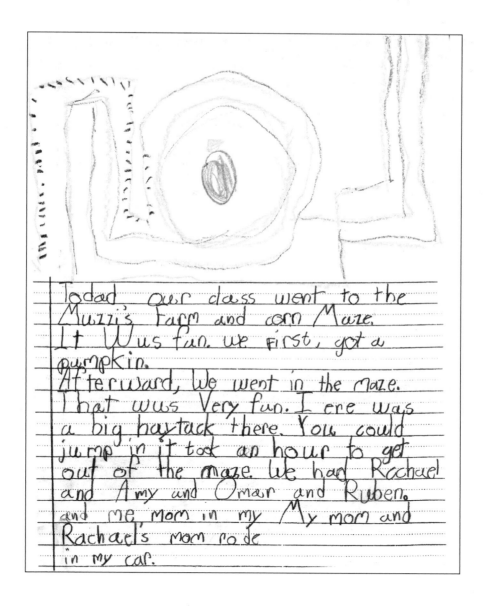

Todad our class went to the
Muzzi's farm and corn Maze.
It wus fun. We First, got a
pumpKir.
Afterward, We went in the maze.
That wus Very fun. There was
a big haytack there. You could
jump in it took an hour to get
out of the maze. We had Rachael
and Amy and Omar and Ruben.
and me, mom in my My mom and
Rachael's mom rode
in my car.

# Score Point 2 *continued*

## Assessment Summary: "The cone mazze"

| ELEMENTS | | |
|---|---|---|
| | **Needs Instruction** | **Commentary** |
| **Orientation and Context** | • Establishes a simple context (e.g., time, place, or occasion). | The writer creates a context by beginning with the sentence, "Todad, our class went to the Muzzi's Farm and corn Maze." |
| **Plot Development and Organization** | • Produces writing that is typically framed by initiating and closing incidents, though the sequence may not be clear. | The piece describes many of the events of the field trip (such as getting pumpkins, entering the maze, and playing in a haystack), but the sequence of events is not clear. For instance, the reader moves from discussing the maze to the carpool, but the shift in topic is hard to follow, and the connection between the two events is not clear. |
| **Character/ Narrator Development** | • Typically provides little, if any, character development. | |
| **Closure** | • May simply stop.<br>• May provide a simple evaluative comment (e.g., "It was fun."). | The piece simply stops. |
| STRATEGIES | | |
| | **Needs Instruction** | **Commentary** |
| **Detail** | • Produces writing that contains few details. | |
| **Dialogue** | • May attempt the use of dialogue. | |
| **Other** | • May use some simple form of literary language.<br>• Uses simple transition words and phrases.<br>• Frequently incorporates drawings. | The writer uses transition words such as "First" and "Afterward" to help create coherence. |

*Note: The commentary highlights the elements and strategies in the student paper, focusing on how well the paper addresses the totality of the elements and strategies rather than on whether each is included.*

## Next Steps in Instruction

The writer will benefit from instruction on ordering and elaborating on events and developing character by adding information about the character's internal thoughts, feelings, and motivations.

# Score Point 1

## Narrative Student Work and Commentary:
## "Me and my Dad made a tank..."

Me and my Dad made a tank it is yellow and black. we worked on it for 2 days it was fun makeing a tank.

This is a very short piece with a single event (making the tank), some detail (color of the tank and length of time spent making the tank), and a reflection ("it was fun").

The only orientation to this piece is the writer's announcement that he and his dad made a tank.

The piece is so brief that the initiating event (making the tank) and the closing event (it took two days) are separated by only a description of the tank.

The piece does not include character development.

A simple evaluative comment concludes the piece ("it was fun makeing a tank.").

The writer provides a drawing to accompany the text.

This piece does not include dialogue, literary language, or transitional elements.

Score Point **1** *continued*

## Assessment Summary:
## "Me and my Dad made a tank..."

| ELEMENTS | | |
| --- | --- | --- |
| | **Needs Substantial Support** | **Commentary** |
| **Orientation and Context** | • Establishes a simple context (e.g., time, place, or occasion). | The only orientation to this piece is the writer's announcement that he and his dad made a tank. |
| **Plot Development and Organization** | • Produces writing that is typically framed by initiating and closing incidents, though the sequence may not be clear.<br>• Typically lists, but does not develop, incidents or events. | The piece is so brief that the initiating event (making the tank) and the closing event (it took two days) are separated by only a description of the tank. |
| **Character/ Narrator Development** | • Typically provides little, if any, character development. | |
| **Closure** | • May simply stop.<br>• May provide a simple evaluative comment (e.g., "It was fun."). | A simple evaluative comment concludes the piece ("it was fun making a tank."). |
| STRATEGIES | | |
| | **Needs Substantial Support** | **Commentary** |
| **Detail** | • Produces writing that contains little or no detail. | |
| **Dialogue** | • Typically does not attempt the use of dialogue. | |
| **Other** | • May use some simple form of literary language.<br>• Uses simple transition words and phrases.<br>• Frequently incorporates drawings. | The writer provides a drawing to accompany the text. |

*Note: The commentary highlights the elements and strategies in the student paper, focusing on how well the paper addresses the totality of the elements and strategies rather than on whether each is included.*

## Roadmap for Development

This piece is so brief that if it is at all typical of what the writer habitually produces, it argues for extensive work on fluency. The writer will need time and support to understand story structure and the use of detail. But first of all, work needs to be done to help the writer generate more text.

# Report of Information

Reports of information describe the way things are in the social and natural world. They describe classes of things, but also the components or parts of things and their relations. Reports contain various kinds of information. They answer questions such as, What are the major food groups? What is the earth made of? What role do planets play in the solar system? Reports also give information about aspects of things. They answer questions about size (How big is Texas? How tall is the Eiffel Tower?), about function (What is a telescope used for? What is a modem used for?), about behavior (What do pelicans do to find food? How do whales eat?), and about the organization of systems (What is the relationship of the House to the Senate? How is the court system organized?). Writers of this genre typically make meaning by describing and classifying things and their distinctive features. For children, this often means writing about the features of different kinds of dinosaurs, insects, planes, pets, whales, and so on. When children study science, their reports may deal with different kinds of energy, different kinds of clouds, different types of cells, etc.

Report writing poses many challenges for young students. Writing about a topic that they know well presents a different set of challenges than writing about a topic that is unfamiliar. When students know the topic, organizing the information is the primary task that consumes their energy. When they do not know the topic, gathering and phrasing the information present additional challenges.

When students are writing about a topic they are familiar with, they can convey information in their own words and cluster information in categories that make sense to them. When they do not know the topic, they may not have the breadth or depth of understanding to analyze and categorize the information effectively. In these cases, young writers often seem to rely almost solely on headers, provided either by the teacher or by the reference materials themselves, to organize their writing.

When students do not know the topic, simply phrasing the information can be a daunting task. They must explain new information that they may not fully understand. So, the logical thing for them to do is to borrow heavily from the wording in reference books to make sure they convey correctly the ideas they are writing about. Logically, then, the syntactic patterns that emerge under these circumstances frequently are made up of some introductory, transitional, or evaluative phrasings that string together word-for-word borrowings from reference books. This is called "patch" writing and it is particularly acceptable and expected in the primary grades, where students are encouraged to mimic the language of written texts, to apprentice themselves to authors and to borrow stylistic techniques they observe professional writers using.

The New Standards expectation for student writers in the report genre requires that they be able to craft a report that does the following: establishes a context; creates an organizing structure appropriate to audience and purpose; communicates ideas, insights, or theories that are illustrated through facts, details, quotations, statistics, and other information; uses a range of appropriate strategies to develop the text; and provides closure.

## Orientation and Context

As it relates to report writing, orienting the reader usually means providing some kind of opening statement locating the subject of the paper in the universe of things. For children, the opening statement often takes the form of a definition or classification ("Whales are mammals."). Alternatively, opening statements will sometimes provide an overview of the topic ("There are many different types of whales in the ocean.") or a comment on the organization of a system ("There are three branches in the government of the United States."). Young writers also often attempt to engage reader interest in the topic by introducing startling facts or by appealing to the reader in some fashion.

## Organization of Information

In reports, facts are often grouped into topic areas in a hierarchical pattern of organization such as classification. Reports also describe patterns of relations among concepts linked to facts. Although reports are often considered neutral and voiceless, in reality they convey human agendas or points of view. Thus, effective reports have a controlling idea or perspective that contributes to the organization and coherence of the text. That is, information is selected and ordered in a way that contributes to the development of the idea. Organizing information in a report also requires writers to attend to the needs of their audience by providing the background information a reader would need to understand subsequent portions of the text. Writers also use paragraphing, subheads, transition words, and phrases and clauses to organize the information.

## Development and Specificity of Information

There is a wide variety of ways to report information. Writers define things ("Corn is a vegetable."), give examples ("Dogs are man's best friend. Guide dogs help blind people."), and provide reasons ("My mom works on computers…I know why, she's an engineer."). Writers also explain phenomena ("Atoms are the insides of crystals…. Crystals get flat faces because the atoms form regular patterns inside."). They compare ("Some crystals are like flowers."; "Gray rabbits look like ash and smoke.") and they contrast ("Some crystals grow from lava and some grow from sea salt."). They relate cause and effect ("We used to have a dog, but my dad left the door open and he ran out into the street."). They describe ("Dolphins have a sharp and pointed face."). They specify ("I learned a lot from doing this report. I learned about different types of dogs and breeds."). They evaluate ("All crystals are different and that's what makes them so wonderful."). The different strategies

that writers use can vary from a single sentence to a chunk of text several sentences long.

In developing information in a report, effective writers provide adequate and specific information about the topic. They usually write in the present tense and exclude information that is extraneous or inappropriate. They communicate ideas, insights, and theories that are elaborated on or illustrated by facts, details, quotations, statistics, or other information. Their language is factual and precise, rather than general and non-specific. They use clear and precise descriptive language to convey distinctive features (such as shape, size, color), components (such as parts of a machine, players on a team), behaviors (such as behaviors of animals: birthing, mating, eating), uses (such as uses of soap: washing hair, washing clothes, washing cars). Frequently, writers use specialized vocabulary specifically related to the topic (such as "pride," "cubs," and "dominant male" in a paper about lion families).

Many young writers pick topics from their everyday lives that they are knowledgeable about and that lend themselves to everyday vocabulary (such as siblings, family members, the family dog). In these cases, the writing may appear less sophisticated than the writing of a student who has picked a topic that lends itself to the use of technical vocabulary. But when students work with less familiar topics, the language they use may not appear to be their own. Both situations, in their own way, make it difficult to accurately evaluate the writer's development. It is important to keep in mind, though, that young writers who are imitating the language of the books they read are in the process of making that language their own.

## Closure

Although their reports may not always have a formal conclusion, as would be expected in the writing of adults, young writers typically provide some sort of closure, such as a shift from particular facts to some kind of general statement or claim about the topic ("Everything is an adventure when you have a passport. All you have to do is get one!").

## Report of Information in Second Grade

Like most children, second graders love to tell people about what they know. They write reports on a variety of subjects. Some subjects are familiar from their day-to-day lives. Others are from books they have read or topics they have studied in school. Nevertheless, second graders vary widely in their mastery of this genre.

Less able writers may report information about a topic, but fall far short of creating a coherent report. They may shift randomly from topic to topic or provide irrelevant information ("Rockets are the best things to see what's in space. And hooever invented rocket's is very famese like the first pirsen to be on the moon. But that pirsen is dead."). They may provide a concluding sentence, or they may provide none at all. Their control of the language features of the genre is also unstable. Some young writers at this grade level shift abruptly between timeless statements about a category that are typical of reports ("Raccoons take naps in trees and live in branches.") and comments about specific events or occasions that happened in the past and that are more typical of narratives ("I saw a raccoon in a tree by the apartments.... It didn't see me but I saw it climb the tree.").

Students who meet the standard at second grade usually produce some kind of an introduction ("I'm going to tell you about all the plants."). They create an obvious organizational structure that may be patterned after chapter book headings, picture books, question-and-answer books, etc. They report adequate and specific information and facts about a topic. They often use everyday vocabulary to write about topics with which they are familiar in their everyday experience ("My mom"), but they are also beginning to use specialized vocabulary in their reports about topics that they have encountered in their reading ("The moon has many phases. I will tell you them one by one. They are the New Moon, Waxing Crescent, First Quarter, Waxing Gibbous, Last Quarter, Waning Crescent, and Old Moon."). Students who meet the standard at second grade may include illustrations or graphics to support their texts, and they provide a concluding section or statement ("I wrote this report because I like the moon a lot!").

# Report of Information Rubrics Elements

|  | **5**<br>**Exceeds Standard\*** | **4**<br>**Meets Standard** |
|---|---|---|
| **Orientation and Context** | • Usually produces some kind of introduction (e.g., "I'm going to tell you about all the plants."). | • Usually produces some kind of introduction (e.g., "I'm going to tell you about all the plants."). |
| **Organization of Information** | • Creates an obvious organizational structure (e.g., may be patterned after chapter book headings, picture books, question-and-answer books). | • Creates an obvious organizational structure (e.g., may be patterned after chapter book headings, picture books, question-and-answer books). |
| **Development and Specificity of Information** | • Reports adequate and specific facts and information pertinent to the topic.<br>• Communicates elaborated ideas, insights, or theories through facts, concrete details, quotations, statistics, or other information. | • Reports adequate and specific facts and information pertinent to the topic.<br>• Communicates elaborated ideas, insights, or theories through facts, concrete details, quotations, statistics, or other information. |
| **Closure** | • Usually provides a concluding sentence or section. | • Usually provides a concluding sentence or section. |

|  | **3**<br>**Needs Revision** | **2**<br>**Needs Instruction** | **1**<br>**Needs Substantial Support** |
|---|---|---|---|
| **Orientation and Context** | • May produce some kind of introduction.<br>• May use only the title to introduce the topic. | • May produce some kind of introduction.<br>• May use only the title to introduce the topic. | • Typically uses only the title to introduce the topic. |
| **Organization of Information** | • May create an organizational structure (e.g., loosely grouped information). | • Attempts an organizational structure (e.g., may include an introduction and conclusion but not group information consistently). | • Attempts to organize text (e.g., does not group information consistently or includes irrelevant information). |
| **Development and Specificity of Information** | • Reports facts and information about the topic.<br>• Provides some details pertinent to the topic. | • Reports facts and information about the topic.<br>• Provides some details pertinent to the topic. | • Reports facts and information about the topic.<br>• Provides few details. |
| **Closure** | • Usually provides a concluding sentence or section. | • May provide a concluding sentence. | • May simply stop. |

\*The criteria that define score points 5 and 4 are identical. This is intentional. What distinguishes a 5 from a 4 is not the presence or absence of a particular element or strategy. Rather, it is the overall quality of execution and the level of language the writer employs. Writers of score point 5 papers bring something to the text that may not be provided by instruction—a deep understanding or passion for the topic and the genre.

# Report of Information Rubrics Strategies

| | 5<br>Exceeds Standard* | 4<br>Meets Standard |
|---|---|---|
| **Names and Vocabulary** | • Uses names and specialized vocabulary specific to the topic. | • Uses names and specialized vocabulary specific to the topic. |
| **Other** | • May include illustrations or graphics to support the text. | • May include illustrations or graphics tzo support the text. |

| | 3<br>Needs Revision | 2<br>Needs Instruction | 1<br>Needs Substantial Support |
|---|---|---|---|
| **Names and Vocabulary** | • Uses names and specialized vocabulary related to the topic. | • Uses names and vocabulary related to the topic. | • Uses names and vocabulary related to the topic. |
| **Other** | • May include illustrations or graphics to support the text. | • May include illustrations or graphics to support the text. | • May attempt to use illustrations or graphics to support the text. |

*The criteria that define score points 5 and 4 are identical. This is intentional. What distinguishes a 5 from a 4 is not the presence or absence of a particular element or strategy. Rather, it is the overall quality of execution and the level of language the writer employs. Writers of score point 5 papers bring something to the text that may not be provided by instruction—a deep understanding or passion for the topic and the genre.

# Score Point 5

## Report of Information Student Work and Commentary: "Facts About Cats!"

"Facts About Cats!" is a carefully organized piece that discusses types of cats and caring for cats. The piece exceeds the standard for second grade.

The writer introduces the subject by identifying cats as mammals and describing their characteristics in general ("They can have long or short, straight or wavy hair. They have retractable claws.").

This piece has an obvious organizational structure. Facts and details are clustered around subtopics (characteristics of breeds, characteristics as pets, how to care for cats). Shifts from one section of the piece to the next are signaled with transition sentences. For instance, at the end of the section on different breeds, the sentence, "A good mother cat would feed, clean and snuggle her babies" serves as a transition to the next section, which deals with the good and bad characteristics of cats as pets.

The writer provides facts and specific descriptive details to describe distinguishing features of three different breeds (White Persian: "thick, soft long hair with a fluffy tail"; Manx: "it has no tail! Also, its back legs are longer than its front legs"; Calico: "black, brown and orange patches on its white fur").

In a concluding section, the writer personalizes the report by writing about her own cat, named Blue. She tells readers that Blue "likes to sleep with my great-grandmother Ree, who it about 93 years old. They keep each other company."

The piece includes specialized vocabulary related to the topic ("predators," "retractable claws," and "Manx").

The writer's drawings support and add to her text. For instance, her drawings of the different breeds illustrate their distinguishing characteristics. For the section on caring for cats, her drawings illustrate the kinds of things an owner would need to do.

# Score Point 5 *continued*

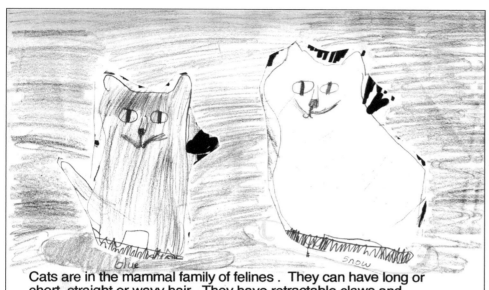

Cats are in the mammal family of felines . They can have long or short, straight or wavy hair . They have retractable claws and sharp teeth because they are predators . There are many different kinds of cats.

The White Persian cat has thick , soft long hair with a fluffy tail. It can have orange, copper or blue eye, and sometime two different color at the same time ! This is a loving pet because it will keep you warm while you hold it and it is also very impressive!

# Score Point 5 *continued*

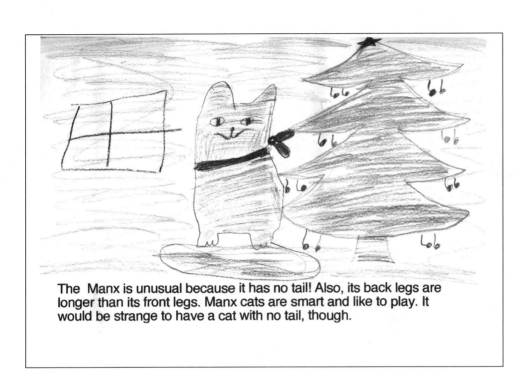

The Manx is unusual because it has no tail! Also, its back legs are longer than its front legs. Manx cats are smart and like to play. It would be strange to have a cat with no tail, though.

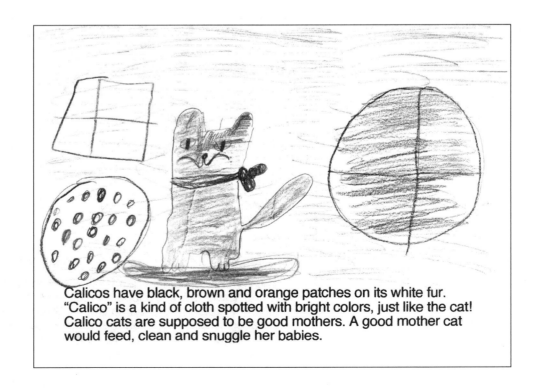

Calicos have black, brown and orange patches on its white fur. "Calico" is a kind of cloth spotted with bright colors, just like the cat! Calico cats are supposed to be good mothers. A good mother cat would feed, clean and snuggle her babies.

# Score Point 5 *continued*

Some cats make good pets for families. They cuddle with people, they are gentle and give comfort to lonely people. Other cats are not the best pets because they scratch people, wander off or fight with other household cats.

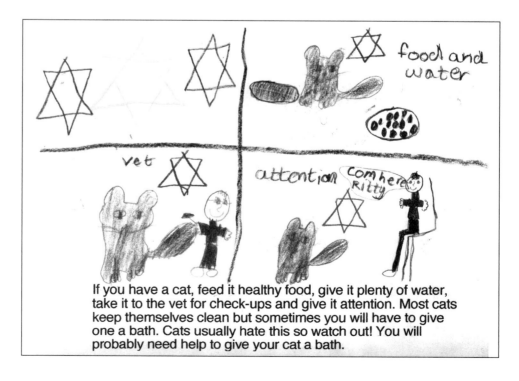

If you have a cat, feed it healthy food, give it plenty of water, take it to the vet for check-ups and give it attention. Most cats keep themselves clean but sometimes you will have to give one a bath. Cats usually hate this so watch out! You will probably need help to give your cat a bath.

# Score Point 4

## Report of Information Student Work and Commentary: "ALL ABOUT THE MOON!"

"ALL ABOUT THE MOON!" provides readers with specific information about the moon, including a discussion of the moon's phases and craters and facts about astronauts on the moon. This piece is an example of a strong paper at score point 4 for second grade.

The writer introduces the topic by contradicting a well-known myth about the moon ("Some people think the moon is made of green cheese....well is's NOT!"). The introduction also previews the next section of the report about the phases of the moon ("The moon has many phases, I will tell you them one by one.").

In general, similar information is presented together in this piece (such as the phases of the moon, craters on the moon, astronauts on the moon).

The writer provides several facts and specific details ("you can see 30,000 craters" and "The year the first astronauts from Earth went to the moon was in 1969.") and communicates elaborated ideas and theories ("The phases are made by the reflection of the sun hitting the moon in different places.").

The writer wraps up his report with a concluding sentence that explains why he wrote the report ("I wrote this report because I like the moon a lot!").

The piece includes vocabulary that is uniquely related to the topic ("New Moon, Waxing Crescent, First Quarter, Waxing Gibbous").

The piece includes drawings that illustrate the phases of the moon for readers.

# Score Point 4 *continued*

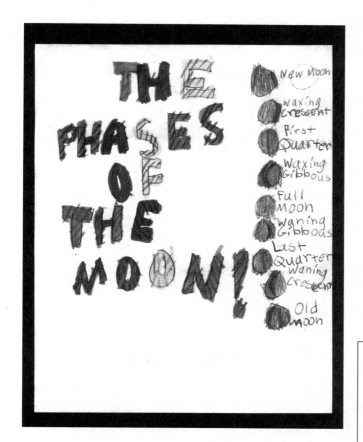

All About The Moon!
Some people think the moon
is made of green cheese.... well
is's NOT! The moon has many
phases, I will tell you them one
by one. They are the New Moon
Waxing Crescent, First Quarter,
Waxing Gibbous, Last Quarter,
Waning Crescent, and Old
Moon. The phases are made
by the reflection of the sun hitting

# Score Point 4 *continued*

the moon in different places.
Many craters have not been
named by astronauts.
With a small telescope you
can see 30,000 craters on the
moon. The year the first
astronauts from Earth went
to the moon was in 1969,
A footprint from an astronaut
will stay on the moon for thousands
of years because there is no wind or rain

to blow or wash it away.
I wrote this report because
I like the moon a lot!

# Score Point 4 *continued*

## Assessment Summary: "ALL ABOUT THE MOON!"

| ELEMENTS | | |
|---|---|---|
| | **Meets Standard** | **Commentary** |
| **Orientation and Context** | • Usually produces some kind of introduction (e.g., "I'm going to tell you about all the plants."). | The writer introduces the topic by contradicting a well-known myth about the moon ("Some people think the moon is made of green cheese....well is's NOT!"). The introduction also previews the next section of the report about the phases of the moon ("The moon has many phases, I will tell you them one by one."). |
| **Organization of Information** | • Creates an obvious organizational structure (e.g., may be patterned after chapter book headings, picture books, question-and-answer books). | In general, similar information is presented together in this piece (such as the phases of the moon, craters on the moon, astronauts on the moon). |
| **Development and Specificity of Information** | • Reports adequate and specific facts and information pertinent to the topic.<br>• Communicates elaborated ideas, insights, or theories through facts, concrete details, quotations, statistics, or other information. | The writer provides several facts and specific details ("you can see 30,000 craters" and "The year the first astronauts from Earth went to the moon was in 1969.") and communicates elaborated ideas and theories ("The phases are made by the reflection of the sun hitting the moon in different places."). |
| **Closure** | • Usually provides a concluding sentence or section. | The writer wraps up his report with a concluding sentence that explains why he wrote the report ("I wrote this report because I like the moon a lot!") |

| STRATEGIES | | |
|---|---|---|
| | **Meets Standard** | **Commentary** |
| **Names and Vocabulary** | • Uses names and specialized vocabulary specific to the topic. | The piece includes vocabulary that is uniquely related to the topic ("New Moon, Waxing Crescent, First Quarter, Waxing Gibbous"). |
| **Other** | • May include illustrations or graphics to support the text. | The piece includes drawings that illustrate the phases of the moon for readers. |

*Note: The commentary highlights the elements and strategies in the student paper, focusing on how well the paper addresses the totality of the elements and strategies rather than on whether each is included.*

# Score Point 3

## Report of Information Student Work and Commentary: "---'s Book About Dogs"

In "---'s Book About Dogs," the writer provides readers with facts about dogs. The writer has created an organizational structure, but the sections often lack sufficient detail. This piece needs revision in order to meet the standard for second grade.

The writer uses only the title of the piece to introduce the topic.

This piece has some internal organization noting that the information is loosely grouped with separate topics appearing on each page (what dogs eat and drink, what all dogs have in common, different kinds of dogs, dog behavior, where dogs live).

The writer includes some general information about dogs ("some dogs are furry, while some are just plain bald"), but the various topics and points are not supported with specific details.

The writer concludes the piece by summing up her feelings about dogs: "Dogs can be intaresting, fun, and great!"

The writer uses some vocabulary specifically related to the topic ("mammals," "pack").

The piece includes drawings that illustrate the writer's points about dogs (such as a drawing of cats and dogs together).

# Score Point 3 *continued*

Some dogs like dry food But some others like canned. food. Wild dogs most always eat meat. Lots of dogs drink water, but barely any dogs drink milk without spitting it up.

# Score Point 3 *continued*

There are diffrent kinds of dogs. For example, there are dalmations and labs. All dogs are mammals wich means every dog in the world is world is warm blooded, it has hair (like poodle or fur, and it has babies called puppies

# Score Point 3 *continued*

Dogs play with cats a lot. Dogs growl when they are mad they could bite you so you better watch out! Dogs bark when they are happy to see you or when they are not familear with you.

# Score Point 3 *continued*

Some dogs are furry, while some are just plain bald. Black labs have blue skin underneath their fur. Did you know that?

# Score Point 3 continued

Some dogs live in a dog house, while some really lucky dogs get to live in your house! Dogs that live in the wild live in packs. A pack is a group of dogs that lives together.

# Score Point 3 *continued*

## Score Point 3 *continued*

# Assessment Summary: "---'s Book About Dogs"

| ELEMENTS | | |
|---|---|---|
| | **Needs Revision** | **Commentary** |
| **Orientation and Context** | • May produce some kind of introduction.<br>• May use only the title to introduce the topic. | The writer uses only the title of the piece to introduce the topic. |
| **Organization of Information** | • May create an organizational structure (e.g., loosely grouped information). | This piece has some internal organization noting that the information is loosely grouped with separate topics appearing on each page (what dogs eat and drink, what all dogs have in common and different kinds of dogs, dog behavior, where dogs live). |
| **Development and Specificity of Information** | • Reports facts and information about the topic.<br>• Provides some details pertinent to the topic. | The writer includes some general information about dogs ("some dogs are furry, while some are just plain bald"), but the various topics and points are not supported with specific details. |
| **Closure** | • Usually provides a concluding sentence or section. | The writer concludes the piece by summing up her feelings about dogs: "Dogs can be intaresting, fun, and great!" |
| STRATEGIES | | |
| | **Needs Revision** | **Commentary** |
| **Names and Vocabulary** | • Uses names and specialized vocabulary specific to the topic. | The writer uses some vocabulary specifically related to the topic ("mammals," "pack"). |
| **Other** | • May include illustrations or graphics to support the text. | The piece includes drawings that illustrate the writer's points about dogs (such as a drawing of cats and dogs together). |

*Note: The commentary highlights the elements and strategies in the student paper, focusing on how well the paper addresses the totality of the elements and strategies rather than on whether each is included.*

## Possible Conference Topics

The writer will benefit from a conference to discuss introducing a topic, adding specific facts and information and elaborating on the topic by explaining the importance of the information provided, and grouping information in related categories.

# Score Point 2

## Report of Information Student Work and Commentary: "all about Racoons"

The writer of "all about Racoons" reports information about a topic, but he will need substantial instruction in order to meet the standard for second grade.

The writer mistakenly uses the title and cover page to announce the topic, and he attempts to introduce his report on raccoons by reporting his experience seeing one: "I saw a raccoon in a tree by the apartments."

The writer attempts an organizational structure, including an introduction and a simple conclusion ("The End"). After telling about his encounter with the raccoon, the writer shifts without transition to statements about raccoons in general (what they eat and where they live).

Several facts are presented; for the most part, the piece is made up of single sentences that are presented in more or less random order ("Raccoons take naps in trees and live in branches. Their fuzzy fur is smooth. They swim, climb, and have fun together. They hunt."). Some details are provided, but in general, subtopics are not well developed.

The piece concludes with the phrase "The End."

The piece includes drawings of raccoons to illustrate the information the writer presents, but the drawings are not always consistent with the details the writer provides. The first drawings (of raccoons climbing trees) are generally consistent with what is said in the text. The drawing of a raccoon sleeping in a tree may introduce confusion, since the raccoon appears to be sleeping on a pillow.

# Score Point 2 *continued*

Raccoons

I saw a raccoon in a tree by the apartments. I was black and white. It was cute. It did'nt see me but I saw it climb the tree. It was eating food, it was grapes. Raccoons eat Cray fish and its a favorite treat. Raccoons eat Nuts, acorng berries, fruits, crabs, frogs

fish. Raccoons take naps in trees and live in branches. Their fuzzy fur is smooth. They swim, climb, and have fun together. They hunt. And walk like Bears. Their favorite place is the pond. They like to play in it. Their temperure drops. Early they March

# Score Point 2 *continued*

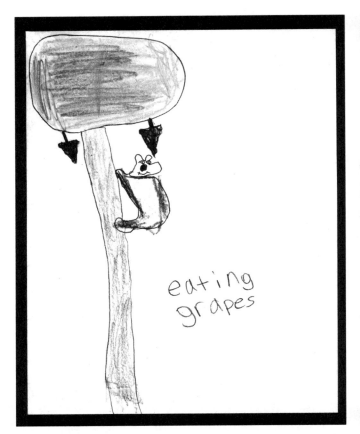

eating
grapes

Slepping
in a tree

The
End

## Score Point 2 *continued*

# Assessment Summary: "all about Racoons"

| ELEMENTS | | |
|---|---|---|
| | **Needs Instruction** | **Commentary** |
| **Orientation and Context** | • May produce some kind of introduction.<br>• May use only the title to introduce the topic. | The writer mistakenly uses the title and cover page to announce the topic. The writer attempts to introduce his report on raccoons by reporting his experience seeing one: "I saw a raccoon in a tree by the apartments." |
| **Organization of Information** | • Attempts an organizational structure (e.g., may include an introduction and conclusion but not group information consistently). | The writer attempts an organizational structure, including an introduction and a simple conclusion ("The End"). After telling about his encounter with the raccoon, the writer shifts without transition to statements about raccoons in general (what they eat and where they live). |
| **Development and Specificity of Information** | • Reports facts and information about the topic.<br>• Provides some details pertinent to the topic. | Several facts are presented; for the most part, the piece is made up of single sentences that are presented in more or less random order ("Raccoons take naps in trees and live in branches. Their fuzzy fur is smooth. They swim, climb, and have fun together. They hunt."). Some details are provided, but in general, subtopics are not well developed. |
| **Closure** | • May provide a concluding sentence. | The piece concludes with the phrase "The End." |

| STRATEGIES | | |
|---|---|---|
| | **Needs Instruction** | **Commentary** |
| **Names and Vocabulary** | • Uses names and vocabulary related to the topic. | |
| **Other** | • May include illustrations or graphics to support the text. | The piece includes drawings of raccoons to illustrate the information the writer presents, but the drawings are not always consistent with the details the writer provides. The first drawings (of raccoons climbing trees) are generally consistent with what is said in the text. The drawing of a raccoon sleeping in a tree may introduce confusion since the raccoon appears to be sleeping on a pillow. |

*Note: The commentary highlights the elements and strategies in the student paper, focusing on how well the paper addresses the totality of the elements and strategies rather than on whether each is included.*

## Next Steps in Instruction

The writer will benefit from instruction on introducing a topic, creating an organizational structure, and elaborating on information by providing facts, quotations, or other information.

# Score Point 1

## Report of Information Student Work and Commentary: "Talking about Rockets"

The writer of "Talking about Rockets" will need substantial support and instruction in order to meet the standard. The writer provides few facts and only one detail that is a wildly inaccurate exaggeration of the height of rocket stands, even those rockets that need "very big stands" ("liKe the 5,000,000,000,9000 Feet high"). Also, the piece includes pictures of several fanciful things that are not mentioned or explained in the text (such as a spaceship and an astronaut's arm holding a suction cup).

The writer mistakenly uses the title to introduce the topic.

The information is not grouped consistently ("they [rockets] need to be big. Jest like tranes.").

The information provided in this text is highly imaginative ("They [rockets] have restrents and toylets and sleeping areause and snaks."). The piece includes a drawing of the imaginary rocket the student describes.

There is no conclusion.

The piece does not include specialized vocabulary.

At times, the drawings support the text.

# Score Point 1 continued

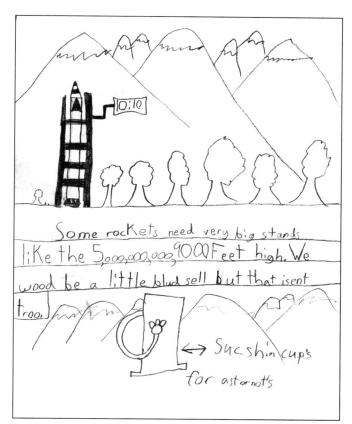

Some rockets need very big stands like the 5,000,000,000,9000 Feet high. We wood be a little blud sell but that isent troo.

→ Sucshin cup's for astornot's

Rockets are the best thing's to see what's in space. And hoo ever invented rockets is very famese like the first pirsen to be on the moon. But that pirsen is ded.

◁ the spaship in the picture

# Score Point 1 *continued*

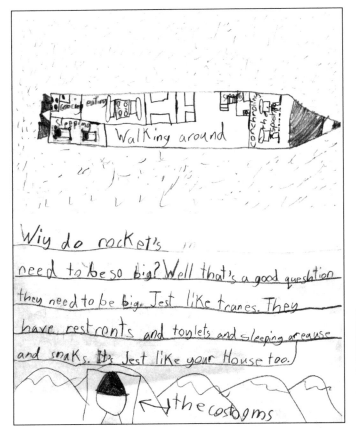

Walking around

Wiy do rockets
need to be so big? Well that's a good queshtion
they need to be big. Jest like tranes. They
have restronts and toylets and sleeping areause
and snaks. It's Jest like your House too.

the costogms

billding a rocket

sumn prople and Kids want to bescientists. And want
to bild rockets. And its a very cool thing for Kids.

Score Point 1 *continued*

## Assessment Summary: "Talking about Rockets"

| ELEMENTS | | |
|---|---|---|
| | **Needs Substantial Support** | **Commentary** |
| **Orientation and Context** | • Typically uses only the title to introduce the topic. | The writer mistakenly uses the title to introduce the topic. |
| **Organization of Information** | • Attempts to organize text (e.g., does not group information consistently or includes irrelevant information). | The information is not grouped consistently ("they [rockets] need to be big. Jest like tranes."). |
| **Development and Specificity of Information** | • Reports facts and information about the topic.<br>• Provides few details. | The information provided in this text is highly imaginative ("They [rockets] have restrents and toylets and sleeping areause and snaks."). |
| **Closure** | • May simply stop. | The piece simply stops. |

| STRATEGIES | | |
|---|---|---|
| | **Needs Substantial Support** | **Commentary** |
| **Names and Vocabulary** | • Uses names and vocabulary related to the topic. | |
| **Other** | • May attempt to use illustrations or graphics to support the text. | At times, the drawings support the text. The piece includes a drawing of the imaginary rocket the student describes. |

*Note: The commentary highlights the elements and strategies in the student paper, focusing on how well the paper addresses the totality of the elements and strategies rather than on whether each is included.*

## Roadmap for Instruction

This writer needs a substantial amount of instruction in basic sentence structure and mechanics. Additionally, the writer might benefit from instruction on the difference between fact and fiction, particulary the different genre elements and rhetorical strategies used in reports of information.

# Instructions

Instructions (sometimes called procedures, functional writing, or process essays) tell readers how to do something or describe how something is done through a sequence of actions. Beverly Derewianka (1990) explains that this genre is very important in our society because it makes it possible for us to get things done. There are many subgenres of this kind of writing: appliance manuals, science experiments, craft instructions, recipes, directions to reach a destination or to build a model, game rules, etc. In school, this type of writing appears frequently in science, homemaking, art, and other classes that focus on processes as opposed to things.

Instructions are like narratives because they are basically chronological in structure; however, instructions describe steps in a process instead of events in time. Because they are chronological in structure, children who write narratives can easily learn how to organize this genre. Young writers usually have little, if any, difficulty sequencing the steps in a plan of action.

Instructions require students to have expertise they can draw on. Fortunately, students have much expertise, even at the primary level. They know how to play games, care for pets, carve pumpkins, make peanut butter sandwiches, and so on. Having something to write about is not a problem for children who write this genre. However, the degree of specificity required sometimes makes writing instructions difficult, as does the problem of engaging the reader. Very young writers will sometimes adopt a narrative stance, presenting steps as actions they take or have taken ("I plant a sed [seed]. I water my sed [seed]. I wat far a rot [waited for a root].") But when students see good examples of instructions, and model their own text on the examples, they are less likely to simply recount. Some topics are simply much more difficult for young writers than others. Topics that are too broad or detailed (for instance, how to play soccer, how to build a model car) are often too difficult for students, especially for those whose writing generally does not meet the standard.

## Orientation and Context

There is no single way to begin instructions, but at the very least, writers must identify the activity or process and the goal. Writers of this genre also provide context, both in the beginning and throughout the text. They may explain why actions are necessary or why steps have to be taken in a particular order. They may include comments on the significance, usefulness, entertainment value, or danger of the activity in order to engage the reader. Typically, young writers of this genre also establish their credentials. That is, they create a knowledgeable stance. In texts by adult writers of this genre, a knowledgeable stance is often assumed. In the case of young writers, pictures may play a large role in providing both context and essential information.

## Organization and Development of Instructions

Like narratives, instructions are organized by time. But instead of events, steps in a process or activity are the deep structure for organization. The text is organized by a sequence of actions. Typically, writers begin with the first step in the process and proceed in time until the last step. Goals are identified, materials are listed, typically in order of use, and steps oriented toward achieving the goal are described.

Writers elaborate on and organize steps in the process in a variety of ways (for example, by providing diagrams, giving reasons for actions, and creating visual imagery through words and illustrations). They create expectations through the use of predictable structures. Headings, subheadings, numbers, etc. are often used to make the process easy to understand and follow. Because instructions are organized by steps in time, common linking words are used (before, during, after, first of all, finally, next, later, simultaneously, subsequently, immediately following, in the meantime). Writers also use transition phrases to make their instructions clear and easy to follow ("When you're all done with that..."). The reader is typically referred to in a general way (one/you), but sometimes the reader is not mentioned at all if the writer uses commands to signal the steps to take ("Take the top off the hamster cage.").

When writing in this genre, successful writers provide a specific guide to action (or a specific description of the activity). They describe the steps or key components in detail, anticipating a reader's need for information and foreseeing likely points of confusion. They explain what to do, and how and why to do it ("Always try to give your hamster food at the same time each day. Then they can learn how to get up at the same time each day."). Sometimes they comment on who would need to know how to do the activity. They explain precautions that should be taken and warn about possible difficulties. They anticipate places where problems are likely to occur ("Food bowl heavy enough so the hamster can't pick it up"; "Don't give them citrus fruits, Onions, or garlic.").

Effective writers of this genre provide specific details (to explain how, what, where, and when), and they adjust the level of detail to fit the goal. They use diagrams or illustrations as complements and to supplement the verbal information in the text. They describe materials, tools, and preparations needed to carry out the process, providing precise information about size, length, weight, number, types, and so on. They define technical terms and explain steps in the process.

## Closure

Often the last step of the process is the conclusion of the writing. Although instructions may not always have a formal conclusion, writers typically provide some sort of closure. Sometimes writers explain the significance of the process or summarize the main steps. Young writers sometimes use a simple concluding statement to say how one could use the results if the process leads to a product ("Maybe if you make enough you can sell them to people..."). Sometimes they simply exhort the reader to engage in the activity ("Now that you know something about Wakeboarding, get out their and wakeboard!").

## Instructions in Second Grade

When they write instructions, most second graders will organize the steps to be followed in appropriate order. Less able writers, however, may not. They may fail to include essential steps, and they may not provide enough detail for the reader to understand the procedure. They may rely on the title to introduce the topic, and they typically provide few details. Some writers at this grade level may even cast steps in the past tense, recounting the experience as if it is something they have done. These less able writers may provide a sense of completeness, if not closure.

Writers who meet the standard at this grade level provide a context and identify the topic. Some will also attempt to engage the reader by using humor, a question, etc. ("What sport has a truck, a tail, a nose and rails?? Skateboarding!"; "I know how to ride a bike. Would you like to ride a bike too?!"). They provide step-by-step instructions that are appropriately sequenced, using sentences that are direct and explanatory, and they include sufficient detail so that the reader can understand what to do ("Then you get two eggs out of the refrigerator. Crack the two eggs one by one in the bowl."). They include relevant information and may elaborate on actions by including significant and specific details ("Get up some good speed on a half-pipe ramp. Try to reach 20 mph."). They signal the sequence of steps with simple transition words ("First," "next," "third," "After that"), and they use language that is straightforward and clear. They frequently use pictures to illustrate steps in the procedure. They may also warn readers about potential problems ("This can cause rail damage to the rail and steps, so be careful."; "Then if you are going to crash turn or push your pedals back.").

Finally, they use a variety of techniques to provide closure to their pieces. A favorite strategy is to suggest reasons and rewards for doing it ("Finally you can eat your brownies with your family."; "Now you can relax and enjoy your lemonade and yourself!").

# Instructions Rubrics Elements

|  | 5<br>Exceeds Standard* | 4<br>Meets Standard |
|---|---|---|
| **Orientation and Context** | • Introduces the topic.<br>• Establishes a context.<br>• Engages the reader.<br>• May convey a knowledgeable stance. | • Introduces the topic.<br>• Establishes a context.<br>• Engages the reader.<br>• May convey a knowledgeable stance. |
| **Organization and Development of Instructions** | • Provides step-by-step instructions that are appropriately sequenced.<br>• Provides sufficient detail for the reader to understand the instructions. | • Provides step-by-step instructions that are appropriately sequenced.<br>• Provides sufficient detail for the reader to understand the instructions. |
| **Closure** | • Provides closure. | • Provides closure. |

|  | 3<br>Needs Revision | 2<br>Needs Instruction | 1<br>Needs Substantial Support |
|---|---|---|---|
| **Orientation and Context** | • Introduces the topic.<br>• Establishes a context.<br>• Engages the reader.<br>• May convey a knowledgeable stance. | • Announces the topic. | • May announce the topic only with the title. |
| **Organization and Development of Instructions** | • Provides very general instructions.<br>• Organizes steps or actions in order by time.<br>• May provide insufficient detail for the reader to understand the instructions. | • May provide only a simple list of unelaborated steps.<br>• May provide steps or actions that are out of sequence or too general to follow.<br>• Provides insufficient detail for the reader to understand the instructions. | • May provide only a very simple list of unelaborated steps.<br>• May provide steps or actions that are out of sequence or too general to follow.<br>• May omit important steps.<br>• Provides insufficient detail for the reader to understand the instructions.<br>• May cast steps in past tense. |
| **Closure** | • Provides closure. | • Provides closure. | • May provide a sense of completeness, if not closure. |

*The criteria that define score points 5 and 4 are identical. This is international. What distinguishes a 5 from a 4 is not the presence or absence of a particular element or strategy. Rather, it is the overall quality of execution and the level of language the writer employs. Writers of score point 5 papers bring something to the next that may not be provided by instruction—a deep understanding or passion for the topic and the genre.

# Instructions Rubrics Strategies

|  | 5<br>**Exceeds Standard\*** | 4<br>**Meets Standard** |
|---|---|---|
| **Transition Devices** | • Uses simple transition words (e.g., first, after, next) or other devices (e.g., headings, question and answer) to indicate sequence of steps or actions.<br>• May number the steps or actions. | • Uses simple transition words (e.g., first, after, next) or other devices (e.g., headings, question and answer) to indicate sequence of steps or actions.<br>• May number the steps or actions. |
| **Other** | • May use drawings or graphics to illustrate instructions. | • May use drawings or graphics to illustrate instructions. |

|  | 3<br>**Needs Revision** | 2<br>**Needs Instruction** | 1<br>**Needs Substantial Support** |
|---|---|---|---|
| **Transition Devices** | • Uses simple transition words to indicate sequence of steps or actions (e.g., first, after, next).<br>• May number the steps or actions. | • Uses simple transition words to indicate sequence of steps or actions (e.g., first, after, next).<br>• May number the steps or actions. | • Uses simple transition words to indicate sequence of steps or actions (e.g., first, after, next).<br>• May number the steps or actions. |
| **Other** | • May use drawings or graphics to illustrate instructions. | • May use drawings or graphics to illustrate instructions. | • May use drawings or graphics to illustrate instructions. |

\*The criteria that define score points 5 and 4 are identical. This is international. What distinguishes a 5 from a 4 is not the presence or absence of a particular element or strategy. Rather, it is the overall quality of execution and the level of language the writer employs. Writers of score point 5 papers bring something to the next that may not be provided by instruction—a deep understanding or passion for the topic and the genre.

# Score Point 5

## Instructions Student Work and Commentary: "Skateboarding!"

Skateboarding!

"Skateboarding!" exceeds the standard for writing instructions in second grade. The writer has organized this delightful piece around a series of riddles and questions, and he answers his riddles by providing facts about skateboarding and instructions on how to skate.

The piece engages the reader and introduces the topic with a riddle ("What sport has a truck, a tail, a nose and rails??"). The page that follows provides the answer ("Skateboarding!"), as well as definitions of the skating terms "truck," "tail," "nose," and "rail" ("The truck connects the board to the wheels.") and a diagram of a skateboard.

The writer conveys a knowledgeable stance by using and explaining vocabulary specific to skateboarding (such as "truck" and "tail").

The piece's creative organizational structure engages the reader and provides the writer with many opportunities to tell the reader about skateboarding. The piece continues with a series of riddles that ask and answer questions about skateboarding and provide readers with instructions for moves such as "How To Do A McTwist" and "How to Move Forward."

The writer provides specific guides to action for each stunt, and he elaborates on actions by including significant details for readers ("Get up some good speed on a half-pipe ramp. Try to reach 20 mph.").

In "How to Stop," the writer elaborates on the topic and demonstrates his expertise by giving different instructions for "Beginner," "Middler" and "Advanced (like me)" skaters.

The last page of the piece asks and answers the question, "Where can skate-boarders go so people won't try to get rid of them?" Although the writer does not provide a formal closure to the piece, the question-and-answer format gives the piece a sense of completeness.

The directions for each skateboarding stunt are numbered and organized by time. The directions include transition words, phrases, and clauses to help guide the reader through the process ("When you get up to speed…"; "At the same time…").

The writer uses page layout to create suspense by asking his riddles on one page and giving readers the answers on the page that follows.

# Score Point 5 *continued*

What sport has a truck, a tail, a nose and rails? ?

Skateboarding !
The truck connects the board to the wheels. The back
end of the board is the tail and the front is the nose.
The rails are the sides of the board.

# Score Point 5 *continued*

In what sport do you hold something onto your feet while standing on one hand?

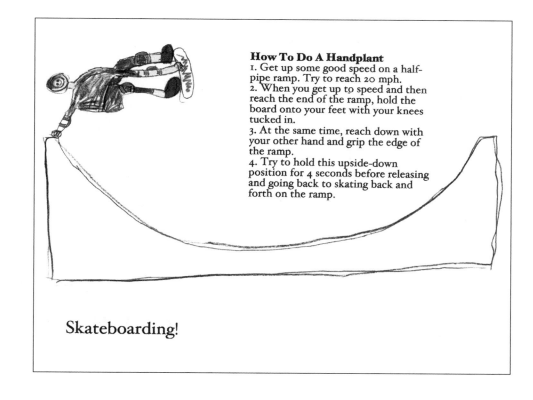

**How To Do A Handplant**
1. Get up some good speed on a half-pipe ramp. Try to reach 20 mph.
2. When you get up to speed and then reach the end of the ramp, hold the board onto your feet with your knees tucked in.
3. At the same time, reach down with your other hand and grip the edge of the ramp.
4. Try to hold this upside-down position for 4 seconds before releasing and going back to skating back and forth on the ramp.

Skateboarding!

# Score Point 5 *continued*

Is a McTwist a new sandwich at McDonald's?

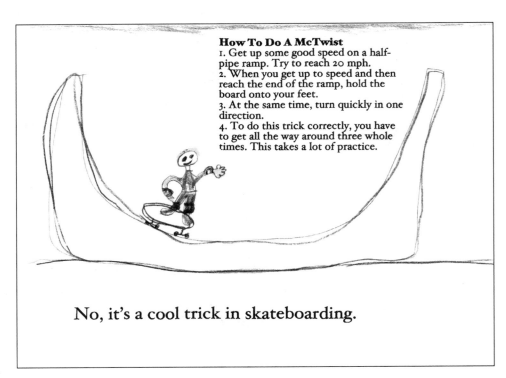

**How To Do A McTwist**
1. Get up some good speed on a half-pipe ramp. Try to reach 20 mph.
2. When you get up to speed and then reach the end of the ramp, hold the board onto your feet.
3. At the same time, turn quickly in one direction.
4. To do this trick correctly, you have to get all the way around three whole times. This takes a lot of practice.

No, it's a cool trick in skateboarding.

# Score Point 5 *continued*

What are the basics of skateboarding?

<u>How to Move Forward</u>: Stand with your left foot right below the nose of the board. Kick three times with your right foot to get up speed. After you get moving quickly, reposition your feet as shown in the picture above.

# Score Point 5 *continued*

How to Turn: Apply slight pressure to kick to get the nose into the air. Move the nose either to the left or right before bringing the nose back to the ground.

How to Stop:
1. Beginner: Crash into something hard!
2. Middler: Crash into something soft!
3. Advanced (like me): Lift your left leg up so that your weight causes the tail of the board to drag. This will slow you down.

# $\mathcal{S}$core $\mathcal{P}$oint **5** *continued*

<u>Can you do a nosegrind without getting a scab?</u>
Yes. You grind on only the front truck, usually
along a rail or steps. This can cause damage to the
rail and steps, so be careful.

<u>Where can skate-boarders go so people won't try to
get rid of them?</u>
Many cities have skateboarding parks, where skaters
can do tricks, learn new stuff and just have fun.

Score Point **5** *continued*

# Assessment Summary: "Skateboarding!"

| ELEMENTS | | |
|---|---|---|
| | **Exceeds Standard** | **Commentary** |
| **Orientation and Context** | • Introduces the topic.<br>• Establishes a context.<br>• Engages the reader.<br>• May convey a knowledgeable stance. | The piece engages the reader and introduces the topic with a riddle ("What sport has a truck, a tail, a nose and rails??"). The page that follows provides the answer ("Skateboarding!"), as well as definitions of the skating terms "truck," "tail," "nose," and "rail" ("The truck connects the board to the wheels.") and a diagram of a skateboard. The writer conveys a knowledgeable stance by using and explaining vocabulary specific to skateboarding (such as "truck" and "tail"). |
| **Organization and Development of Instructions** | • Provides step-by-step instructions that are appropriately sequenced.<br>• Provides sufficient detail for the reader to understand the instructions. | The piece's creative organizational structure engages the reader and provides the writer with many opportunities to tell the reader about skateboarding. The piece continues with a series of riddles that ask and answer questions about skateboarding and provide readers with instructions for moves such as "How To Do A McTwist" and "How to Move Forward." The writer provides specific guides to action for each stunt, and he elaborates on actions by including significant details for readers ("Get up some good speed on a half-pipe ramp. Try to reach 20 mph."). In "How to Stop," the writer elaborates on the topic and demonstrates his expertise by giving different instructions for "Beginner," "Middler" and "Advanced (like me)" skaters. |
| **Closure** | • Provides closure. | The last page of the piece asks and answers the question, "Where can skate-boarders go so people won't try to get rid of them?" Although the writer does not provide a formal closure to the piece, the question-and-answer format gives the piece a sense of completeness. |
| STRATEGIES | | |
| | **Exceeds Standard** | **Commentary** |
| **Transition Devices** | • Uses simple transition words (e.g., first, after, next) or other devices (e.g., headings, question and answer) to indicate sequence of steps or actions.<br>• May number the steps or actions. | The directions include transition words, phrases, and clauses to help guide the reader through the process ("When you get up to speed..."; "At the same time...").<br>The directions for each skateboarding stunt are numbered and organized by time. |
| **Other** | • May use drawings or graphics to illustrate instructions. | The writer uses page layout to create suspense by asking his riddles on one page and giving readers the answers on the page that follows. |
| *Note: The commentary highlights the elements and strategies in the student paper, focusing on how well the paper addresses the totality of the elements and strategies rather than on whether each is included.* | | |

# Score Point 4

## Instructions Student Work and Commentary: "Brownies"

> Brownies
>
> If you want to make brownies follow these inportant instructions.
>
> First you get the Brownie Mix Box out on the table.
>
> Second get a big bowl out of a cupboard or shelf.
>
> Third open the Brownine Mix box and yet the powder out of it. pour the powder in the bowl.
>
> After that get a measuring cup

"Brownies" is a good example of a second-grade student's ability to write instructions. The piece meets the standard for second grade.

The writer introduces the topic and provides a general context for the piece ("If you want to make Brownies follow these important instructions.").

The writer provides appropriately sequenced step-by-step instructions for making brownies. The writer uses sentences that are direct and explanatory, and she provides sufficient detail to allow the reader to know what to do ("<u>Then</u> you get two eggs out of the refrigerator. Crack the two eggs one by one in the bowl."). Also, the writer provides specific details ("pour ¼ cups of oil").

The writer concludes her piece with a sentence that describes the joy of completing the steps she describes ("Finally you can eat your brownies with your family!").

The piece includes transition words and phrases to order the different steps in the procedure ("First," "Third," and "After that"), and each transition word is underlined for emphasis.

The piece includes pictures that illustrate the steps the writer describes.

# Score Point 4 continued

and pour freash water
to ¼ cups. Next you
pour the water in the
mesuring cup in the bowl
fild with powder.
Afterthat pour ¼ cups of oil.
Then you get two eggs out of
the refrigcrator. Cradk the
two eggs one by one in the
bowl. There should be a
white plastic bag in the
brownie mix box. Take it

Then you sqeeze it.
out and sopenze it! Soon
choclate should be coming
out. Then stir the bowl with
a large spoon. When
it is all smooth and ready
pour it in a cooking pan.
Put the cookingpan in
the oven for twenty-eight to
thirty minutes. After
that you take the cooking pan
out of the oven.
Now you cut sqause with a nife.

Finally you can eat your
brownies with your family!

Score Point 4 *continued*

## Assessment Summary: "Brownies"

| ELEMENTS | | |
|---|---|---|
| | **Meets Standard** | **Commentary** |
| **Orientation and Context** | • Introduces the topic.<br>• Establishes a context.<br>• Engages the reader.<br>• May convey a knowledgeable stance. | The writer introduces the topic and provides a general context for the piece ("If you want to make Brownies follow these important instructions."). |
| **Organization and Development of Instructions** | • Provides step-by-step instructions that are appropriately sequenced.<br>• Provides sufficient detail for the reader to understand the instructions. | The writer provides step-by-step instructions for making brownies. The writer uses sentences that are direct and explanatory, and she provides sufficient detail to allow the reader to know what to do ("<u>Then</u> you get two eggs out of the refrigerator. Crack the two eggs one by one in the bowl."). Also, the writer provides specific details ("pour ¼ cups of oil"). |
| **Closure** | • Provides closure. | The writer concludes her piece with a sentence that describes the joy of completing the steps she describes ("Finally you can eat your brownies with your family!"). |
| STRATEGIES | | |
| | **Meets Standard** | **Commentary** |
| **Transition Devices** | • Uses simple transition words (e.g., first, after, next) or other devices (e.g., headings, question and answer) to indicate sequence of steps or actions.<br>• May number the steps or actions. | The piece includes transition words and phrases to order the different steps in the procedure ("First," "Third," and "After that"), and each transition word is underlined for emphasis. |
| **Other** | • May use drawings or graphics to illustrate instructions. | The piece includes pictures that illustrate the steps the writer describes. |

*Note: The commentary highlights the elements and strategies in the student paper, focusing on how well the paper addresses the totality of the elements and strategies rather than on whether each is included.*

# Score Point 3

## Instructions Student Work and Commentary: "Thirsty for the best lemonade in town?"

"Thirsty for the best lemonade in town?" approaches the standard for writing instructions in second grade. Although the writer outlines a series of steps for making lemonade, the piece lacks sufficient detail.

The writer announces the topic with the title and the note, "The recipe makes six glasses of lemonade."

The piece begins by providing a context for readers and explaining why readers should make lemonade ("If it's a hot day and you are thirsty and you have no icea what to have. Well I'll teach you how to make the best lemonade in town.").

The piece includes a list of all the necessary materials (such as "Seven rip lemons") and six steps for making lemonade.

The writer uses language that is direct and explanatory, but the piece lacks sufficient detail,

such as information about using the lemon squeezer ("Cut seven lemons in half with the knife put one on the squeezer take it off when all the lemon juice is out.").

The writer closes her piece by encouraging readers to enjoy their lemonade ("There you have it the best lemonade in town! Now you can relax, and enjoy your lemonade and yourself!").

The writer numbers the steps and organizes them by time, and the numbered steps help guide readers through the procedure, though the piece does not include transition words.

The piece provides illustrations to help guide the reader through the process, including pictures of whole lemons and a family enjoying cups of lemonade.

# Score Point 3 *continued*

If it's a hot day and you are thirsty and you have, no idea what to have. Well I'll teach you how to make the best lemonade in town.

materials: Seventin demons, a little cup of sugar. Som ice water, one teaspoon, a lemon squeezer, six cups, and a knife.

1. Cut seven lemons in half with the knife put one on the squeezer take it off when all the lemon juice is out repeal with the rest of lemons.

2 Pour the lemon juice in the cups.

3 Put one teaspoon of sugar in the cups.

4. Pour some ice water in the cups.

5 Stir well with teaspoon

6 Put away the lemon slices, the little cup of sugar, ice water, teaspoon the lemon squeezer, and the knife.

There you have it the best lemonade in town! Now you can relax, and enjoy your lemonade and yourself!

Score Point **3** *continued*

# Assessment Summary:
# "Thirsty for the best lemonade in town?"

| ELEMENTS | | |
| --- | --- | --- |
| | **Needs Revision** | **Commentary** |
| **Orientation and Context** | • Introduces the topic.<br>• Establishes a context.<br>• Engages the reader.<br>• May convey a knowledgeable stance. | The writer announces the topic with the title and the note, "The recipe makes six glasses of lemonade." The piece begins by providing a context for readers and explaining why readers should make lemonade ("If it's a hot day and you are thirsty and you have no icea what to have. Well I'll teach you how to make the best lemonade in town."). |
| **Organization and Development of Instructions** | • Provides very general instructions.<br>• Organizes steps or actions in order by time.<br>• May provide insufficient detail for the reader to understand the instructions. | The piece includes a list of all the necessary materials (such as "Seven rip lemons") and six steps for making lemonade. The writer uses language that is direct and explanatory, but the piece lacks sufficient detail, such as information about using the lemon squeezer ("Cut seven lemons in half with the knife put one on the squeezer take it off when all the lemon juice is out."). |
| **Closure** | • Provides closure. | The writer closes her piece by encouraging readers to enjoy their lemonade ("There you have it the best lemonade in town! Now you can relax, and enjoy your lemonade and yourself!"). |
| STRATEGIES | | |
| | **Needs Revision** | **Commentary** |
| **Transition Devices** | • Uses simple transition words to indicate sequence of steps or actions (e.g., first, after, next).<br>• May number the steps or actions. | The writer numbers the steps and organizes them by time, and the numbered steps help guide readers through the procedure. |
| **Other** | • May use drawings or graphics to illustrate instructions. | The piece includes illustrations to help guide the reader through the process, including pictures of whole lemons and a family enjoying cups of lemonade. |

*Note: The commentary highlights the elements and strategies in the student paper, focusing on how well the paper addresses the totality of the elements and strategies rather than on whether each is included.*

## Possible Conference Topics

The writer will benefit from a conference to discuss adding detail and elaborating on actions, and anticipating and addressing the reader's need for information.

# Score Point 2

## Instructions Student Work and Commentary: "How To Make A Plant"

Language
Writing

How To Make A Plant

This is what you need to make your own little plant seeds, a buket of water, a medium size brown pot, and some black durt for your plant. First, you get your brown pot. Then, you put some of the black durt into the pot. After that, you put two seeds in the durt. Finally, you pour some water into the pot. And then, four a few days it grows until it's big. I like to make my own plant.

"How To Make a Plant" reveals a writer who needs instruction in order to meet the standard for second grade. The piece includes some of the elements of instructions (supply list, series of steps, concluding statement), but the writer does not provide a context or include significant detail.

The writer announces the topic by listing the supplies her readers will need ("This is what you need to make your own little plant seeds..."), but she does not provide a context for the information.

The writer describes how to "make a plant" by providing readers with a simple list of unelaborated steps that are organized by time ("Then, you put some of the black durt into the pot. After that, you put two seeds in the durt."). She includes some descriptive words (such as "black durt" and "medium size brown pot"), but she also omits important details (such as the type of seeds or how much water).

The writer includes a sentence that provides closure ("I like to make my own plant.").

Throughout the piece, the writer uses transition words and phrases to guide readers through the steps ("First," "Then," "After that").

The writer does not include drawings or other graphics to illustrate the instructions.

# Score Point 2 *continued*

## Assessment Summary: "How To Make A Plant"

| ELEMENTS | | |
|---|---|---|
| | **Needs Instruction** | **Commentary** |
| **Orientation and Context** | • Announces the topic. | The writer announces the topic by listing the supplies her readers will need ("This is what you need to make your own little plant seeds."), but she does not provide a context for the information. |
| **Organization and Development of Instructions** | • May provide only a simple list of unelaborated steps.<br>• May provide steps or actions that are out of sequence or too general to follow.<br>• Provides insufficient detail for the reader to understand the instructions. | The writer describes how to "make a plant" by providing readers with a simple list of unelaborated steps that are organized by time ("Then, you put some of the black durt into the pot. After that, you put two seeds in the durt."). She includes some descriptive words (such as "black durt" and "medium size brown pot"), but she also omits important details (such as the type of seeds or how much water). |
| **Closure** | • Provides closure. | The writer includes a sentence that provides closure ("I like to make my own plant."). |

| STRATEGIES | | |
|---|---|---|
| | **Needs Instruction** | **Commentary** |
| **Transition Devices** | • Uses simple transition words to indicate sequence of steps or actions (e.g., first, after, next).<br>• May number the steps or actions. | Throughout the piece, the writer uses transition words and phrases to guide readers through the steps ("First," "Then," "After that"). |
| **Other** | • May use drawings or graphics to illustrate instructions. | The writer does not include drawings or other graphics to illustrate the instructions. |

*Note: The commentary highlights the elements and strategies in the student paper, focusing on how well the paper addresses the totality of the elements and strategies rather than on whether each is included.*

## Next Steps in Instruction

The writer will benefit from instruction on engaging readers and establishing a context for the instructions and on elaborating on the steps by adding information and detail.

# Score Point 1

## Instructions Student Work and Commentary: "I can play basketball"

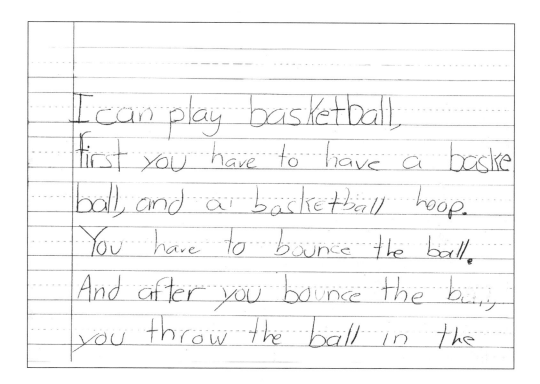

I can play basketball,
first you have to have a baske
ball, and a basketball hoop.
You have to bounce the ball.
And after you bounce the ball,
you throw the ball in the

The author of "I can play basketball" attempts to tell readers how to play basketball. The instructions are very general, and the writer omits important steps and information. The piece does not meet the second-grade standard for writing instructions.

The piece does not include a title.

The writer announces the topic with the sentence "I can play basketball," a statement that seems to indicate that the piece will be a narrative about playing basketball. Despite the misleading opening line, the writer does attempt to provide readers with instructions on how to play basketball.

The piece includes a very simple list of unelaborated actions ("You have to bounce the ball. And after you bounce the ball, you throw the ball in the hoop and you S-C-R-O-E!").

The writer does not include sufficient detail for the reader to be able to understand the activity; she omits important information. For instance, she tells readers, "Which ever teams wins, they get a huge trophy!" but she does not explain how a team wins in basketball.

The writer provides a sense of closure ("And the only thing that is important is…having fun!").

The piece includes simple transition words ("first," "And after…").

# Score Point 1 continued

hoop and you S-C-R-O-E!
And you get a point. Which
ever team wins, they get a huge
huge trophy! You take a rest
or if you want to play again,
then go, do it!
And the only thing that is

important is... having fun!

# Score Point 1 *continued*

# Score Point 1 *continued*

## Assessment Summary: "I can play basketball"

| ELEMENTS | | |
|---|---|---|
| | **Needs Substantial Support** | **Commentary** |
| **Orientation and Context** | • May announce the topic only with the title. | The writer announces the topic with the sentence "I can play basketball," a statement that seems to indicate that the piece will be a narrative about playing basketball. Despite the misleading opening line, the writer does attempt to provide readers with instructions on how to play basketball. |
| **Organization and Development of Instructions** | • May provide only a very simple list of unelaborated steps.<br>• May provide steps or actions that are out of sequence or too general to follow.<br>• May omit important steps.<br>• Provides insufficient detail for the reader to understand the instructions.<br>• May cast steps in past tense. | The piece includes a very simple list of unelaborated actions ("You have to bounce the ball. And after you bounce the ball, you throw the ball in the hoop and you S-C-R-O-E!"). The writer does not include sufficient detail for the reader to be able to understand the activity; she omits important information. For instance, she tells readers, "Which ever teams wins, they get a huge trophy!" but she does not explain how a team wins in basketball. |
| **Closure** | • May provide a sense of completeness, if not closure. | The writer provides a sense of closure ("And the only thing that is important is...having fun!"). |
| STRATEGIES | | |
| | **Needs Substantial Support** | **Commentary** |
| **Transition Devices** | • Uses simple transition words to indicate sequence of steps or actions (e.g., first, after, next).<br>• May number the steps or actions. | The piece includes simple transition words ("first," "And after..."). |
| **Other** | • May use drawings or graphics to illustrate instructions. | |
| *Note: The commentary highlights the elements and strategies in the student paper, focusing on how well the paper addresses the totality of the elements and strategies rather than on whether each is included.* | | |

## Roadmap for Development

The writer has chosen a difficult topic. The rules of basketball are complicated and detailed, and if this student's writing is generally below standard, she will benefit from choosing a less difficult topic. The writer will also benefit from instruction on the elements of instructions, including introducing the topic for readers and providing enough detail so that readers can understand the instructions.

# Response to Literature

The responding to literature genre assessed by New Standards is recognized and assessed in many districts and states throughout the United States, and like other genres, it provides a rough template that defines expectations for a particular kind of writing. But it is important to note that it is only one of several ways that readers and writers respond to literature and only one of several encouraged by teachers in school. Responding to literature can take many different forms. All of them are valuable in a language arts curriculum.

Students may respond in writing to literature in a variety of ways and for a variety of purposes: to express their emotional reactions, clarify their thinking or attitudes, explore difficulties in their understanding, or simply to share their opinions with others to build a social relationship. Teachers sometimes design classroom activities that invite informal, imaginative responses wherein the focus is on helping children make connections to their own experiences and to other texts or authors they have read. Such connections deepen children's understanding.

In the classroom, the development of more formal responses is supported both by these kinds of activities and by Accountable Talk[SM]. Accountable Talk offers a set of tools for helping teachers lead academically productive group discussions. Accountable Talk is not empty chatter; it seriously responds to and further develops what others say, whether the talk occurs one-on-one, in small groups, or with the whole class. When they engage in Accountable Talk, students learn to introduce and ask for knowledge that is accurate and relevant to the text under discussion. They learn to use evidence from the text in ways that are appropriate and follow established norms of good reasoning.

Built on this kind of scaffolding, formal written responses require students to examine texts thoughtfully and to draw evidence from them to make assertions and substantiate arguments. A good response to literature is never built on unsupported opinion. Polished and crafted for an audience, effective papers in this genre always demonstrate a comprehensive understanding of the work, and they persuade readers to accept the writer's interpretation and evaluation of a work of literature by providing evidence.

The New Standards expectations for responding to literature in writing center on this more formal, school-based genre. In the world outside of school, this genre is realized in published reviews of books, poetry, short stories, or other texts. Reviews are judged for the writer's ability to craft effective and defensible commentary—a coherent analysis that is supported by evidence.

The New Standards expectations for student writers in the response to literature genre require that student writers provide an introduction, demonstrate an understanding of the work, advance an interpretation or evaluation, include details from the literature that support the writer's assertions, use a range of appropriate strategies, and provide closure. Supporting judgments with evidence from the text is at the heart of this genre.

## Orientation and Context

There are many ways to introduce a response to a literary work, depending upon the writer's purpose, but introductions usually share some common elements. Context is typically provided, such as the subject of the literature, the identity of the author(s), and the title(s) of the work or works that will be discussed. The writer may also attempt to engage the reader's interest by suggesting a reason for the reader to want to read the literature or by using an attention-grabbing lead. Some writers articulate the main point of their response in the introduction.

## Comprehension, Interpretation, and Evaluation of Literature

The core of a response is the writer's interpretation and evaluation of the literature. Successful writers of this genre make assertions about the work that focus on the important elements of the text. They demonstrate comprehension of the work and a good grasp of the significant ideas of the work or passages in the work. They advance judgments that are interpretive, analytic, evaluative, or reflective, dealing with ambiguities and complexities in the text(s). They deal with questions about motivation, causality, and implications. They typically comment on the author's use of stylistic devices and show an appreciation of the effects created. They make perceptive judgments about the literary quality of the work.

Effective writers of this genre illustrate their interpretations or evaluations of the literature (for example, evaluations of an author's craft, interpretations of a work's theme) with examples or other information about the text. It is common for writers to summarize or paraphrase the work, or relevant parts of it, but successful writers of this genre do not simply retell. They make choices about what to tell the audience and what not to tell, depending upon the points they want to make.

Writers of this genre also sometimes compare and contrast the work they are responding to with other works that they have read or with their own life experiences. They may draw analogies between events or circumstances in literature and events or circumstances in their own lives. In other words, they connect the literature to their life experiences or culture. They support their interpretations or inferences by explaining the characters' motives or the causes of events based on their understanding of people and life in general. They often use quotations to explain and support their interpretation or to illustrate aspects of the author's craft. Used appropriately, quotations add to the credibility of the writer's conclusions.

## Evidence

When students write a formal response to literature, they make a judgment about something they have read or have heard read to them. This judgment can be evaluative ("I liked it because…") or it can be interpretive ("I think the author is saying…"). Successful writers of this genre develop credible arguments to support their judgments. Significantly, this genre requires students to go back into the text to support their evaluation or interpretation. Although reader-response approaches stress the value of individual and unique encounters with text, reader-response theorists do not advocate the idea that every reading of a text is as good as any other. Louise Rosenblatt (1968) says that we must challenge students to be disciplined in the way they work with texts by (1) showing what in the text justifies their response and (2) making clear the criteria or standards of evaluation that they are using.

Because the deep structure of response to literature is argument, usually more than one assertion is put forward, and each is supported by evidence. Individual assertions add weight to the argument and relate back to the writer's overall interpretation or evaluation of the text. In order to make sense of the writer's interpretation or evaluation of a text, the audience needs adequate evidence—examples, details, quotations—along with explanations and reasons. Successful writers of this genre support their interpretations, inferences, and conclusions by referring to the text, other works, other authors, or to personal knowledge. They move beyond purely associative or emotional connections between the literature and their own experience (text-to-self connections) to explain how the connections they write about support their interpretations and evaluations. They convince the reader through logic and with evidence that is both sufficient and relevant. They typically use connecting words associated with reasoning (because, so, the first reason). If they are comparing works, they make accurate and perceptive observations of the similarities and differences between the works, and they support their observations by referring to the texts.

Successful writers of this genre express their feelings and reactions, but they do not overly rely on appeals to emotions or overstate their case. Although young children may often exaggerate or make sweeping generalizations, as they mature, their arguments are more often based on logic and reasoning. Successful writers of this genre do not make hasty generalizations marked by words like "all," "ever," "always," and "never." They qualify their claims, using words like "most," "many," "usually," and "seldom," when such words would be more accurate, and they support their opinions with evidence.

## Closure

Although a response to literature may not always have a formal conclusion, writers typically provide some sort of closure, such as a summing up of the writer's perspective on the work. Writers of this genre often leave the reader with a fresh insight, a quotation, or some other memorable impression.

## Response to Literature in Second Grade

Second graders vary widely in their understanding of the features of the response to literature genre and their ability to write it. For instance, students who have limited understanding of the genre and who struggle with other aspects of writing typically use the book title to introduce the topic ("I read Wilma Unlimited."). They may use simple evaluative expressions to state opinions about the text ("I like it because it's interesting...") and about aspects of the text ("I like the kids because they never argue"), but they provide minimal detail to support their evaluations, and some provide none at all. Some students may provide only a partial retelling, and the retelling is typically not used to support assertions they may make about the text.

Instead of relying on the title of the book for an introduction, students who meet the standard at second grade introduce the topic ("I think this book is about four runaway children."). They may try using catchy lines to engage the reader's interest ("I know what you want, you want to learn about Vera B. Williams."). Students who meet the standard are able to provide a retelling. They may also provide relatively detailed summaries instead of retellings. They make plausible claims about what they have read, for instance, by suggesting a big idea or theme. They make connections between the text and their own ideas and lives. They use evaluative expressions, but they also refer to the text itself when they do so ("there was a very important thing that happened...the fire burned their house"). They give reasons for their evaluations ("I like this book because I think that it is really neat that all of the children can live alone in the wilderness and can cook over an open fire..."). Finally, students who meet the standard support their interpretations with evidence ("this book is also about working together because they all built the swimming pool they all helped with the stew they really work together.").

# Response to Literature Rubrics Elements

| | 5<br>Exceeds Standard* | 4<br>Meets Standard |
|---|---|---|
| **Orientation and Context** | • Typically introduces the topic. | • Typically introduces the topic. |
| **Comprehension, Interpretation, and Evaluation of Literature** | • Demonstrates an understanding of the work(s).<br>• May attempt to articulate a big idea or theme (e.g., "This book is about working together...").<br>• Uses simple evaluative or interpretive expressions to state opinions about the work(s) or parts of the work(s).<br>• Presents response to work(s) in a coherent manner. | • Demonstrates an understanding of the work(s).<br>• May attempt to articulate a big idea or theme (e.g., "This book is about working together...").<br>• Uses simple evaluative or interpretive expressions to state opinions about the work(s) or parts of the work(s).<br>• Presents response to work(s) in a coherent manner. |
| **Evidence** | • Provides a relatively detailed retelling of narrative text (or summary of an informational text).<br>• Provides details to support interpretation or evaluation.<br>• May quote fragments of dialogue when retelling. | • Provides a relatively detailed retelling of narrative text (or summary of an informational text).<br>• Provides details to support interpretation or evaluation.<br>• May quote fragments of dialogue when retelling. |
| **Closure** | • Typically provides closure. | • Typically provides closure. |

*The criteria that define score points 5 and 4 are identical. This is intentional. What distinguishes a 5 from a 4 is not the presence or absence of a particular element or strategy. Rather, it is the overall quality of execution and the level of language the writer employs. Writers of score point 5 papers bring something to the text that may not be provided by instruction—a deep understanding or passion for the topic and the genre.

# Elements *continued*

| | 3<br>Needs Revision | 2<br>Needs Instruction | 1<br>Needs Substantial Support |
|---|---|---|---|
| **Orientation and Context** | • May introduce the topic or may rely on the book title to introduce the topic. | • May introduce the topic or may rely on the book title to introduce the topic. | • Typically relies on the book title to introduce the topic. |
| **Comprehension, Interpretation, and Evaluation of Literature** | • May demonstrate understanding of the work or parts of the work(s).<br>• Makes simple claims about the work(s) or parts of the work(s) (e.g., "The funniest one was when Rosa maks funny face in the mirror.").<br>• Produces a response that may have gaps in coherence. | • May demonstrate literal comprehension of the work or parts of the work(s).<br>• May make simple claims about the work(s) or parts of the work(s) (e.g., "The funniest one was when Rosa maks funny face in the mirror.").<br>• Produces a response that lacks coherence. | • May demonstrate some superficial comprehension of parts of the work(s).<br>• May make simple claims about the work(s) or parts of the work(s) (e.g., "The funniest one was when Rosa maks funny face in the mirror.").<br>• Produces a response that lacks coherence. |
| **Evidence** | • Provides a retelling of the basic story line of narrative text (or a brief summary of an informational text).<br>• May provide relatively few details to support evaluation or interpretation.<br>• May quote fragments of dialogue when retelling. | • May focus on one or two events of a narrative text (or dwell on particular points of information in an informational text).<br>• Provides minimal detail to support evaluation or interpretation.<br>• Typically does not use quotations. | • May focus on one or two events of a narrative text (or on one or two points of information in an informational text).<br>• Provides minimal or no detail to support evaluation.<br>• Typically does not use quotations. |
| **Closure** | • May provide closure. | • May provide closure. | • May provide closure. |

# Response to Literature Rubrics Strategies

| | 5<br>Exceeds Standard* | 4<br>Meets Standard |
|---|---|---|
| **Compare/<br>Contrast** | • If discussing two or more works, describes incidental similarities between them.<br>• May note similarities between the work(s) and their own experiences. | • If discussing two or more works, describes incidental similarities between them.<br>• May note similarities between the work(s) and their own experiences. |
| **Other** | • May refer to literary techniques or concepts (e.g., "I think the theam [theme] of this book is everyone has to go to bed sometime."). | • May refer to literary techniques or concepts (e.g., "I think the theam [theme] of this book is everyone has to go to bed sometime."). |

| | 3<br>Needs Revision | 2<br>Needs Instruction | 1<br>Needs Substantial Support |
|---|---|---|---|
| **Compare/<br>Contrast** | • If discussing two or more works, describes incidental similarities between them.<br>• May note similarities between the work(s) and their own experiences. | • If discussing two or more works, may make comparisons that are general or unclear.<br>• May note similarities between work(s) and their own experiences, but connections may be loose or associative. | • If discussing two or more works, makes comparisons that are typically general or unclear.<br>• May note similarities between work(s) and their own experiences, but connections are typically loose or associative. |
| **Other** | • Typically does not refer to literary techniques or concepts (e.g., theme). | • Typically does not refer to literary techniques or concepts (e.g., theme). | • Typically does not refer to literary techniques or concepts (e.g., theme). |

*The criteria that define score points 5 and 4 are identical. This is intentional. What distinguishes a 5 from a 4 is not the presence or absence of a particular element or strategy. Rather, it is the overall quality of execution and the level of language the writer employs. Writers of score point 5 papers bring something to the text that may not be provided by instruction—a deep understanding or passion for the topic and the genre.

# *Score Point* 5

## Response to Literature Student Work and Commentary: "Response to The Boxcar Children"

> Response to
> The Boxcar Children
> Response
>
> I think this book is about four runaway children. What happens to their parents die and and they think their grandfather is mean. At the beginning of the book on a warm night the children are in front of a bakery They are tierd and hungry. Henry, the oldest buys. some bread and the children eat it. Then they want to sleep there. The bakers wife is mean and dosn't like children but they say that they'll wash dishes if she will let them stay. The bakers wife likes this and lets them stay but in the middle of the night all of the children, but Benny overhear the bakers wife saying To Th; "I'll keep the three older children to wash dish but the little one must go. I cannot take care of him'').
> "Very well, said the baker. I will take him to a orphanage in the morning")
> Well the children don't want to lose Benny so they run away They sleep in some hay on a farm. When they wake up it's night and it's raining too. Not just raining a whole thunderstorm. Then Jesse finds an old boxcar. The children sleep in it because it provides shelter. Then they make it their home! They have alot of adventures in it and build alot of things. This book is about cooperation because the children work together Henry gets the money, Jessie, Benny, and Violet

In "Response to The Boxcar Children," the writer begins by providing a retelling of Gertrude Chandler Warner's *The Boxcar Children* for readers. She continues by discussing some of the themes in the book (such as cooperation and loving each other). This piece exceeds the standard for response to literature in second grade.

The writer introduces the topic by making a statement about the book ("I think this book is about four runaway children.").

The piece continues with a relatively detailed retelling of the book that discusses why the children live in a boxcar (their parents die and they do not want to live with their scary grandfather; they take shelter in a bakery, but run away when they overhear the baker's wife planning to take the youngest child to the orphanage; they find an abandoned boxcar and make it their home). The retelling demonstrates an understanding of the book, but the writer does not recount the orphans' developing relationship with a kindly man or their happy discovery that the man is their grandfather.

The piece is presented in a coherent manner: The writer begins with a retelling, and she continues by discussing the big ideas in the book, drawing comparisons between *The Boxcar Children* and another book, and making connections with her own life.

# Score Point 5 *continued*

Response to The Boxcar Children

find the dishes and bluberries, they all do something important. This book is also about working together because they all built the swimming pool they all helped with the stew they really work together. It's also about loving each other because the children care for each other. Jessie found the boxcar and told the others she didn't just say, "go find somewhere else!" This book reminds me of The Barn because in The Barn the childs parents die too. This book makes me think of when we go camping because we can't use a stove we have to use a fire. We can't sleep in beds we have to sleep in sleeping bags. I like this book because I think that it is really neat that all of the children can live alone in the wilderness and can cook over an open fire and find their own dises and sleep in pine needles and live in a boxcar.

The writer articulates several big ideas in the book, and she uses evidence from the work to support her assertions about them ("This book is about cooperation because the children work together. Henry gets the money, Jessie, Bennie, and Violet find the dishes and the blueberries…"; "This book is also about working together because they all built the swimming pool.").

Throughout the piece, the writer uses examples from the work to support her assertions about it ("It's also about loving each other because the children care for each other. Jessie found the boxcar and told the others she didn't just say, 'go find somewhere else!'").

The writer quotes fragments of dialogue in her retelling of the book ("'Very well, said the baker. I will take him to a orphanage in the morning.'").

The writer closes the piece by stating her opinion about it ("I like this book because I think that it is really neat that all of the children can live alone in the wilderness and can cook over an open fire and find their own dises [dishes] and sleep in pine needles and live in a boxcar.").

The piece includes a comparison between *The Boxcar Children* and Avi's *The Barn* ("This book reminds me of <u>The Barn</u> because in <u>The Barn</u> the children's parents die too.").

The writer notes similarities between the book and her own experience ("This book makes me think of when we go camping because we can't use a stove we have to use a fire.").

 _continued_

# Assessment Summary:
# "Response to <u>The</u> <u>Boxcar</u> <u>Children</u>"

| ELEMENTS | | |
|---|---|---|
| | **Exceeds Standard** | **Commentary** |
| **Orientation and Context** | • Typically introduces the topic. | The writer introduces the topic by making a statement about the book ("I think this book is about four runaway children."). |
| **Comprehension, Interpretation, and Evaluation of Literature** | • Demonstrates an understanding of the work(s).<br>• May attempt to articulate a big idea or theme (e.g., "This book is about working together..."). <br>• Uses simple evaluative or interpretive expressions to state opinions about the work(s) or parts of the work(s).<br>• Presents response to work(s) in a coherent manner. | The piece is presented in a coherent manner: The writer begins with a retelling, and she continues by discussing the big ideas in the book, drawing comparisons between _The Boxcar Children_ and another book, and making connections with her own life. The writer articulates several big ideas in the book, and she uses evidence from the work to support her assertions about them ("This book is about cooperation because the children work together. Henry gets the money, Jessie, Bennie, and Violet find the dishes and the blueberries..."; "This book is also about working together because they all built the swimming pool."). |
| **Evidence** | • Provides a relatively detailed retelling of narrative text (or summary of an informational text).<br>• Provides details to support interpretation or evaluation.<br>• May quote fragments of dialogue when retelling. | The piece includes a relatively detailed retelling of the book that discusses why the children live in a boxcar (their parents die and they do not want to live with their scary grandfather; they take shelter in a bakery, but run away when they overhear the baker's wife planning to take the youngest child to the orphanage; they find an abandoned boxcar and make it their home). The retelling demonstrates an understanding of the book, but the writer does not recount the orphans' developing relationship with a kindly man or their happy discovery that the man is their grandfather.<br><br>Throughout the piece, the writer uses examples from the work to support her assertions about it ("It's also about loving each other because the children care for each other. Jessie found the boxcar and told the others she didn't just say, 'go find somewhere else!'").<br><br>The writer quotes fragments of dialogue in her retelling of the book ("'Very well, said the baker. I will take him to a orphanage in the morning.'"). |
| **Closure** | • Typically provides closure. | The writer closes the piece by stating her opinion about it ("I like this book because I think that it is really neat that all of the children can live alone in the wilderness and can cook over an open fire and find their own dises [dishes] and sleep in pine needles and live in a boxcar."). |

# Score Point 5 *continued*

| STRATEGIES | | |
|---|---|---|
| | **Exceeds Standard** | **Commentary** |
| **Compare/Contrast** | • If discussing two or more works, describes incidental similarities between them.<br>• May note similarities between the work(s) and their own experiences. | The piece includes a comparison between *The Boxcar Children* and Avi's *The Barn* ("This book reminds me of *The Barn* because in *The Barn* the children's parents die too.").<br><br>The writer notes similarities between the book and her own experience ("This book makes me think of when we go camping because we can't use a stove we have to use a fire."). |
| **Other** | • May refer to literary techniques or concepts (e.g., "I think the theam [theme] of this book is everyone has to go to bed sometime."). | |
| *Note: The commentary highlights the elements and strategies in the student paper, focusing on how well the paper addresses the totality of the elements and strategies rather than on whether each is included.* | | |

# Score Point 4

## Response to Literature Student Work and Commentary: "Something Special For Me"

> Something Specical For Me
>
> * Rosa had so many ideas she did not know what to get for her birthday. She cried sad tears. Her mom was kind enough to say "don't worry" I guess trying on skutes, dresses, and looking in a tent store was not good enough for her to spend the jar money! She made a wish and she heard music.

In this response to literature, the writer discusses Vera B. Williams's *Something Special for Me*, and she draws comparisons between *Something Special for Me* and Williams's *A Chair for My Mother*. This piece meets the standard for a response to literature in second grade.

The writer begins by discussing the main conflict in *Something Special for Me* ("Rosa had so many ideas she did not know what to get for her birthday.").

The piece continues with a relatively detailed retelling of the book (Rosa didn't know what to buy for her birthday; she looked and looked for a gift; she was inspired to buy an accordion because her grandmother loves them).

When the writer compares *Something Special for Me* with *A Chair for My Mother*, she uses examples from the books to support her comparisons ("A chair For My Mother ties with Something Special For Me. They are the same family. They save in the same jar. Mama wanted something special for herself and so she got a soft, fat armchair. Rosa also wanted something special and she found an accordian.").

# Score Point 4 *continued*

Then she found
what she wanted — the accordian.
her grandma used to play it
and it made people
feel like the tables
and chairs dance. So
when her mom told Rosa
that her grandma played
it, it made her feel
better. They saved together,
and spent the mony
together. * Vera B. Williams
Wrote two books that tie
together. A chair For
My Mother ties with

The writer concludes the piece by articulating a big idea from the book ("IT IS GREAT TO HAVE A FAMILY!").

The writer draws comparisons between Williams's books and her own life ("I love reading her books about Rosa's family. My family helps me and my brother with our homework.").

# Score Point 4 continued

Something Special For Me.
They are the same
family. They save
in the same jar.
Mama wanted something
special for herself
and so she got a
soft, fat, armchair.
Rosa also wanted something
special and she found
an accordian. She
wanted to play it.
Vera B. Williams is a
great writer. I love
reading her books

about Rosa's family.
My family helps me
and my brother with
our homework.
IT IS GREAT TO
HAVE A FAMILY!

# Score Point 4 continued

## Assessment Summary: "Something Special For Me"

| ELEMENTS | | |
|---|---|---|
| | **Meets Standard** | **Commentary** |
| **Orientation and Context** | • Typically introduces the topic. | The writer begins by discussing the main conflict in *Something Special for Me* ("Rosa had so many ideas she did not know what to get for her birthday."). |
| **Comprehension, Interpretation, and Evaluation of Literature** | • Demonstrates an understanding of the work(s).<br>• May attempt to articulate a big idea or theme (e.g., "This book is about working together..."). <br>• Uses simple evaluative or interpretive expressions to state opinions about the work(s) or parts of the work(s).<br>• Presents response to work(s) in a coherent manner. | The writer's opening statement and retelling of the story demonstrate her understanding of the book. |
| **Evidence** | • Provides a relatively detailed retelling of narrative text (or summary of an informational text).<br>• Provides details to support interpretation or evaluation.<br>• May quote fragments of dialogue when retelling. | The piece includes a relatively detailed retelling of the book (Rosa didn't know what to buy for her birthday; she looked and looked for a gift; she was inspired to buy an accordion because her grandmother loves them).<br>When the writer compares *Something Special for Me* with *A Chair for My Mother*, she uses examples from the books to support her comparisons ("A chair For My Mother ties with Something Special For Me. They are the same family. They save in the same jar. Mama wanted something special for herself and so she got a soft, fat armchair. Rosa also wanted something special and she found an accordian."). |
| **Closure** | • Typically provides closure. | The writer concludes the piece by articulating a big idea from the book ("IT IS GREAT TO HAVE A FAMILY!"). |

| STRATEGIES | | |
|---|---|---|
| | **Meets Standard** | **Commentary** |
| **Compare/ Contrast** | • If discussing two or more works, describes incidental similarities between them.<br>• May note similarities between the work(s) and their own experiences. | The writer discusses similarities between *Something Special for Me* and *A Chair for My Mother*.<br>The writer draws comparisons between Williams's books and her own life ("I love reading her books about Rosa's family. My family helps me and my brother with our homework."). |
| **Other** | • May refer to literary techniques or concepts (e.g., "I think the theam [theme] of this book is everyone has to go to bed sometime."). | |

*Note: The commentary highlights the elements and strategies in the student paper, focusing on how well the paper addresses the totality of the elements and strategies rather than on whether each is included.*

# Score Point 3

## Response to Literature Student Work and Commentary: "Vera B. Williams wrote Three Days On A River..."

Vera B. Williams wrote Three Days On A River In A Red Canoe. This is a book about Aunt Rosie, cousin Sam, Mom and the narrator. I like this book because I learned that at a water fall you have to lower the boat by ropes and that you have to be careful or you will fall out of the boat. When the river ends it becomes a lake, that reminds me of when I was in a canoe with my cousin Sarah and Sarah's stepsister kristin at lake tahoe. My favorite part is at the end where Sixtoes, their cat after midnight is chewing on fish. I like Vera B. Williams because she puts so much details in her writing and lets the characters do nice things not bad

This piece is a response to *Three Days on a River in a Red Canoe* by Vera B. Williams. The piece includes some of the elements of a response to literature (discussion of the text and connections between the text and the writer's life), but the piece lacks coherence. The piece needs revision in order to meet the standard for a response to literature at second grade.

The writer relies on the author and book title to introduce the topic ("Vera B. Williams wrote <u>Three Days On A River In A Red Canoe</u>.").

The writer demonstrates a general understanding of the book. She refers to parts of the work throughout the piece ("This is a book about Aunt Rosie, cousin Sam, Mom and the narrator."), but much of the retelling is included at the end of the piece ("it tells what happened to the canoe like when in the middle of the night the canoe was getting loose because there was a big storm and rapids."). Because the retelling occurs at the end of the piece, the relationships between the events the writer discusses are not always clear.

The writer makes simple evaluative statements about parts of the work ("I like this book because I learned that at a water fall you have to lower the

# Score Point 3 continued

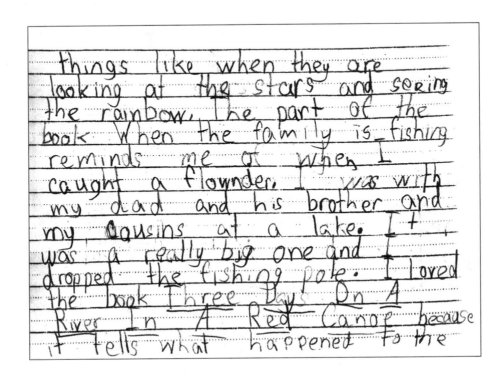

boat by ropes…"; "I loved the book <u>Three Days On A River In A Red Canoe</u> because it tells what happened to the canoe…"; "My favorite part is…").

The response lacks coherence because the writer skips back and forth between her assertions about the book and her connections between the book and her own life (discussions about Williams's craft are immediately followed by a text-to-self connection, which is then followed by a retelling of part of the book).

The piece includes some details that support the writer's assertions about the book ("I like Vera B. Williams because she puts so much details in her writing and lets the characters do nice things not bad things like when they are looking at the stars and seeing the rainbow."). Overall, the focus of this response is on text-to-self connections and simple evaluative statements.

The writer concludes by articulating a big idea in the book ("The important part is the family made it home without getting hurt.").

# Score Point 3 *continued*

canoe like when in the middle of the night the canoe was geting loose because there was a big storm and rapids. The inportend part is the family made it home with out getting hurt.

# Score Point 3 *continued*

## Assessment Summary: "Vera B. Williams wrote Three Days On A River…"

| ELEMENTS | | |
| --- | --- | --- |
| | **Needs Revision** | **Commentary** |
| **Orientation and Context** | • May introduce the topic or may rely on the book title to introduce the topic. | The writer relies on the author and book title to introduce the topic ("Vera B. Williams wrote <u>Three Days On A River In A Red Canoe</u>."). |
| **Comprehension, Interpretation, and Evaluation of Literature** | • May demonstrate understanding of the work or parts of the work(s).<br>• Makes simple claims about the work(s) or parts of the work(s) (e.g., "The funniest one was when Rosa maks funny face in the mirror.").<br>• Produces response that may have gaps in coherence. | The writer demonstrates a general understanding of the book. She refers to parts of the work throughout the piece ("This is a book about Aunt Rosie, cousin Sam, Mom and the narrator."), but much of the retelling is included at the end of the piece ("it tells what happened to the canoe like when in the middle of the night the canoe was getting loose because there was a big storm and rapids."). The writer makes simple evaluative statements about parts of the work ("I like this book because I learned that at a water fall you have to lower the boat by ropes…"; "I loved the book <u>Three Days On A River In A Red Canoe</u> because it tells what happened to the canoe…"; "My favorite part is…"). The response lacks coherence because the writer skips back and forth between her assertions about the book and her connections between the book and her own life (discussions about Williams's craft are immediately followed by a text-to-self connection, which is then followed by a retelling of part of the book). |
| **Evidence** | • Provides a retelling of the basic story line of narrative text (or a brief summary of an informational text).<br>• May provide relatively few details to support evaluation or interpretation.<br>• May quote fragments of dialogue when retelling. | Because the retelling occurs at the end of the piece, the relationships between the events the writer discusses are not always clear. The piece includes some details that support the writer's assertions about the book ("I like Vera B. Williams because she puts so much details in her writing and lets the characters do nice things not bad things like when they are looking at the stars and seeing the rainbow."). Overall, the focus of this response is on text-to-self connections and simple evaluative statements. |
| **Closure** | • May provide closure. | The writer concludes by articulating a big idea in the book ("The important part is the family made it home without getting hurt."). |

# Score Point 3 *continued*

| STRATEGIES | | |
|---|---|---|
| | **Needs Revision** | **Commentary** |
| **Compare/Contrast** | • If discussing two or more works, describes incidental similarities between them.<br>• May note similarities between the work(s) and their own experiences. | The writer makes connections between the book and her own experience throughout the piece ("that reminds me of when I was in a canoe with my cousin Sarah..."). |
| **Other** | • Typically does not refer to literary techniques or concepts (e.g., theme). | |
| *Note: The commentary highlights the elements and strategies in the student paper, focusing on how well the paper addresses the totality of the elements and strategies rather than on whether each is included.* | | |

## Possible Conference Topics

This writer will benefit from a conference to discuss providing a brief retelling of the book to demonstrate understanding and to help readers follow the response, including details from the book to support assertions about it, and revising the piece for coherence (for instance, by including the retelling of the book near the beginning of the response).

# Score Point 2

## Response to Literature Student Work and Commentary: "Response to writing"

Response to writing

The children take care of each other and love each other but they never ever argue. They became very happy together and they build things like fires, pools, and lots of others. They love each other a lot and like each other a lot. When Henry goes to work, they love each other and help each other They like it when Henry goes to work because when Henry comes back from work then he has a fruit or vegetable or money or something else like a hammer or bent nails and lots of others. I think The Boxcar children is compared to The Barn because some kids have to take of their father. The kids have to yell

This response to literature discusses *The Boxcar Children* by Gertrude Chandler Warner. The writer retells parts of the book for readers, but he omits essential information and does not provide examples from the book to support his discussion. This piece does not meet the standard for a response to literature in second grade.

The writer begins by providing a skeletal (and partial) outline of the story line for readers ("The children take care of each other and love each other but they never argue."). Because the writer does not name the author or title of the work, the reader has to infer what book he's discussing.

The writer's recount of the book demonstrates a literal comprehension of parts of the work: He discusses the relationship between the children ("They love each other a lot and like each other a lot.") and Henry's work, but he does not mention that they are orphans struggling for survival or discuss the ending when they discover that Henry's kindly employer is their grandfather.

The piece lacks coherence; the writer focuses on parts of *The Boxcar Children* and often does not provide examples from the book to support his assertions. For instance, he writes, "When Henry goes to work, they love each other and help each other," but

# Score Point 2 continued

Response to writing

at the dad but the dad can't talk so the dad
has to talk with his eyes. I like it because
it's interesting and I like the kids because they
never ever argue.

he does not give examples of how the other children help each other (for instance, they find a blueberry patch and dishes).

The piece concludes with simple evaluative statements about the work ("I like it because it's interesting and I like the kids because they never ever argue.").

The piece includes a comparison with Avi's *The Barn*. The writer provides an anecdote from *The Barn*, but he does not explain how the example he provides relates to *The Boxcar Children* ("I think The Boxcar Children is compared to The Barn because some kids have to take care of their father. The kids have to yell at the dad but the dad can't talk so the dad has to talk with this eyes.").

# *Score Point* 2 *continued*

## Assessment Summary: "Response to writing"

| ELEMENTS | | |
|---|---|---|
| | **Needs Instruction** | **Commentary** |
| **Orientation and Context** | • May introduce the topic or may rely on the book title to introduce the topic. | The writer begins by providing a skeletal (and partial) outline of the story line for readers ("The children take care of each other and love each other but they never argue."). Because the writer does not early on name the author or title of the work, the reader has to infer what book he's discussing. |
| **Comprehension, Interpretation, and Evaluation of Literature** | • May demonstrate literal comprehension of the work or parts of the work(s).<br>• May make simple claims about the work(s) or parts of the work(s) (e.g., "The funniest one was when Rosa maks funny face in the mirror.").<br>• Produces a response that lacks coherence. | The writer's recount of the book demonstrates a literal comprehension of parts of the work: He discusses the relationship between the children ("They love each other a lot and like each other a lot.") and Henry's work, but he does not mention that they are orphans struggling for survival or discuss the ending when they discover that Henry's kindly employer is their grandfather. |
| **Evidence** | • May focus on one or two events of a narrative text (or dwell on particular points of information in an informational text).<br>• Provides minimal detail to support evaluation or interpretation.<br>• Typically does not use quotations. | The piece lacks coherence; the writer focuses on parts of *The Boxcar Children*, and he often does not provide examples from the book to support his assertions. For instance, he writes, "When Henry goes to work, they love each other and help each other," but he does not give examples of how the other children help each other (for instance, they find a blueberry patch and dishes). |
| **Closure** | • May provide closure. | The piece concludes with simple evaluative statements about the work ("I like it because it's interesting and I like the kids because they never ever argue."). |

 *Score Point* **2** *continued*

| STRATEGIES | | |
|---|---|---|
| | **Needs Instruction** | **Commentary** |
| **Compare/Contrast** | • If discussing two or more works, may make comparisons that are general or unclear.<br>• May note similarities between work(s) and their own experiences, but connections may be loose and/or associative. | The piece includes a comparison with Avi's *The Barn*. The writer provides an anecdote from *The Barn*, but he does not explain how the example he provides relates to *The Boxcar Children* ("I think <u>The Boxcar Children</u> is compared to <u>The Barn</u> because some kids have to take care of their father. The kids have to yell at the dad but the dad can't talk so the dad has to talk with this eyes."). |
| **Other** | • Typically does not refer to literary techniques or concepts (e.g., theme). | |
| *Note: The commentary highlights the elements and strategies in the student paper, focusing on how well the paper addresses the totality of the elements and strategies rather than on whether each is included.* | | |

## Next Steps in Instruction

The writer will benefit from instruction on introducing the topic to readers, providing a retelling of the book that demonstrates that the writer understands the book, making interpretive comments about the book, and supporting assertions about the book with examples from the book.

# Score Point 1

## Response to Literature Student Work and Commentary: "Now One Foot Now The Other"

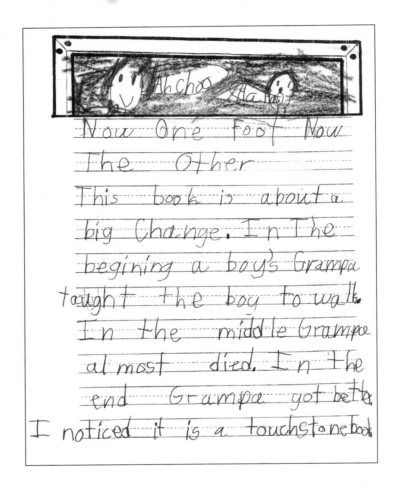

In this piece, the writer gives us a response to Tomie de Paola's *Now One Foot, Now the Other.* The response is framed in terms of what the writer understands: a beginning, a middle, and an end. The text is so brief that it is difficult to gauge the writer's understanding of the book. This piece fails to meet the standard for a response to literature in the second grade.

The writer uses the title of the book to introduce the topic.

The writer makes a claim about (rather than an evaluation of) the book ("This book is about a big Change."), but he does not support the claim with examples from the book. Instead, the writer focuses on three events in the text: one at the beginning, one in the middle, and one at the end ("In The begining a boy's Grampa taught the boy to walk. In the middle Grampa almost died. In the end Grampa got better.").

The writer does not provide details to support his claim about the book.

The writer closes the piece with the following comment: "I noticed it is a touchstone book."

The writer does not make connections between the book and his own experience.

 *continued*

# Assessment Summary:
# "Now One Foot Now The Other"

| ELEMENTS | | |
|---|---|---|
| | **Needs Substantial Support** | **Commentary** |
| **Orientation and Context** | • Typically relies on the book title to introduce the topic. | The writer uses the title of the book to introduce the topic. |
| **Comprehension, Interpretation, and Evaluation of Literature** | • May demonstrate some superficial comprehension of parts of the work(s).<br>• May make simple claims about the work(s) or parts of the work(s) (e.g., "The funniest one was when Rosa maks funny face in the mirror.").<br>• Produces a response that lacks coherence. | The writer makes a claim about (rather than an evaluation of) the book ("This book is about a big Change."). |
| **Evidence** | • May focus on one or two events of a narrative text (or on one or two points of information in an informational text).<br>• Provides minimal or no detail to support evaluation.<br>• Typically does not use quotations. | The writer does not support his claim about the book ("This book is about a big Change.") with examples from the book. Instead, the writer focuses on three events in the text: one at the beginning, one in the middle, and one at the end ("In The begining a boy's Grampa taught the boy to walk. In the middle Grampa almost died. In the end Grampa got better."). |
| **Closure** | • May provide closure. | The writer closes the piece with the following comment: "I noticed it is a touchstone book." |
| STRATEGIES | | |
| | **Needs Substantial Support** | **Commentary** |
| **Compare/ Contrast** | • If discussing two or more works, makes comparisons that are typically general or unclear.<br>• May note similarities between work(s) and their own experiences, but connections are typically loose and/or associative. | |
| **Other** | • Typically does not refer to literary techniques or concepts (e.g., theme). | |

*Note: The commentary highlights the elements and strategies in the student paper, focusing on how well the paper addresses the totality of the elements and strategies rather than on whether each is included.*

## Roadmap for Development

The writer needs to develop understanding about the elements of a formal response to literature, especially about how to introduce a topic and how to provide sufficient and appropriate detail. The text is also markedly short, so the writer quite likely needs time and practice to develop fluency.

# References

Black, P., & Wiliam, D. (1998). Inside the black box: Raising standards through classroom assessment. *Phi Delta Kappan, 80*(2), 139–149.

Bruner, J. (1985). Narrative and paradigmatic modes of thought. In E. Eisner (Ed.), *Learning and teaching the ways of knowing* (pp. 97–115). Chicago: University of Chicago Press.

Cooper, C.R. (1999). What we know about genres, and how it can help us assign and evaluate writing. In C.R. Cooper & L. Odell (Eds.), *Evaluating writing: The role of teachers' knowledge about text, learning, and culture* (pp. 23–52). Urbana, IL: National Council of Teachers of English.

Derewianka, B. (1990). *Exploring how texts work*. Newtown, Australia: Primary English Teaching Association.

Hillocks, G., Jr. (1984). What works in teaching composition: A meta-analysis of experimental treatment studies. *American Journal of Education, 93*(1), 133–170.

Rosenblatt, L. (1968). A way of happening. *Educational Record, 49*, 339–346.